Sailboat Buyer's Guide

Conducting Your Own Survey

Essential Checklist:
What to Know Before You Buy

Karel Doruyter

FineEdge.com

Front cover photo by: Kelly O'Neil
features Gina and Kent Morrow, in their 1999 U20 National Champion,
Mad Dog. www.U20class.org
Back cover and text photos by author unless otherwise noted.
Book design and production: Elayne Wallis & Melanie Haage
Graphics: Sue Athmann and the author
Editor: Elayne Wallis

Library of Congress Cataloging-in-Publication Data

Doruyter, Karel, 1942–
    Sailboat buyers' guide : conducting your own survey /
    by Karel Doruyter.--1st ed.
      p.   cm.
    ISBN 0-938665-72-3 (pbk.)
    1. Sailboats--Purchasing. I. Title.

VM351 D67 1999
623.8'223'0296--dc21   99-050390

FineEdge.com
an imprint of
Fine Edge Productions LLC

Website: FineEdge.com

FINE EDGE
PRODUCTIONS
ANACORTES, WASHINGTON

Foreword

It is sometimes said that the two happiest days of a yachtsman's life are the day he buys a new boat and the day he sells it. While there may be an element of truth to that comment, it probably originated from someone who experienced a lot of costly problems while they were learning about their craft. This happens with new and used boats, automobiles, and even relationships.

Knowing what you are getting involved with beforehand can eliminate many unpleasant surprises. Yet, anyone who is in love can be blind to the faults and blemishes of the object of their affections, defects which may be quite obvious to even the most casual observer.

New and used cars are often referred to as "lemons" after the owner has had a chance to experience the day-in, day-out operation of the vehicle. In most cases, that automobile was bought because it looked good for the price, had the right color, went round the block OK, and the odometer indicated that it had lots of useful life left in it. Aside from kicking the tires and noting any unpleasant odors, the new owner probably made the decision to buy the car purely on his or her intuition. Relationships are frequently created with a similar inspection which manifests itself in a 50% divorce rate.

Perhaps it is just as well that most of us are optimists at heart—after all just about anything can be fixed at a price (except light bulbs). While some people draw up prenuptial agreements, have blood tests done, and take great care in selecting their mates, there are no guarantees that any of this will make you happy.

Buying a used sailboat involves a lot of soul searching and a certain amount of courage. Unless it is required for financing purposes, few people will go to the trouble of getting a really detailed survey which involves hauling the boat out of the water and having a professional surveyor inspect the hull structure, rigging, the onboard systems and safety gear. While it is good to have someone who is not emotionally invested in the boat do the survey, most comments are written as the honest opinion of the surveyor who will not guarantee that the boat is problem-free. Why would he? After all, it is not a perfect world.

Armed with this book, a potential buyer could conduct a very useful inspection of a used boat (or even a new one) as it provides a checklist of items to look at. To someone new to boating, many of the names used in marine terminology are confusing and the glossary will be much appreciated.

The saying goes that a little knowledge is a dangerous thing, yet in my opinion, it's still better than none.

John Guzzwell

John Guzzwell is author of one of the greatest solo circumnavigation stories of all time, *Trekka Round the World.* In 1998 he completed the Single-handed TransPac in *Endangered Species,* a boat he designed and built himself. Guzzwell now makes his home in Seattle where he builds custom boats.

The joy of sailing is calling you!

Table of Contents

Introduction

So you're thinking of buying a sailboat. You've been out on a boat, either with a friend or on a charter, and you have been bitten by the sailing bug. You love the sense of freedom you get as a 42-foot beautiful ketch glides across the bay. The joys of sailing—the lack of people, the wide open water, the solitude, the ever-changing wind, the challenges—this life is calling to you! You're ready to make the plunge!

But wait. Next to a house, buying a sailboat is probably one of the most significant purchases you will make. Before jumping in, you need to ask yourself some crucial questions: How often will I use this boat? Where will I sail (tropics, high latitudes, near home port)? What *exactly* am I going to use it for? It could be you'd be better off renting a boat, which would save you the initial outlay as well as the continuous maintenance cost and mooring expenses. This would also give you the option of trying out different types of vessels, and, with the money you save, you could easily fly to exotic places and charter a vessel when you arrive.

However, if you've thought about all this and you still want a sailboat, it's time to go shopping!

This book is written for consumers who have a basic, working knowledge of sailboats. I have assumed you know the difference between a hull and a galley, but still need some help, for example, on what to look for when inspecting a sailboat's electrical system. When you think about all the things you need to check for when buying a used car, the prospect of evaluating what works and what doesn't on a sailboat can be daunting. This book is designed as a checklist to assist you in what to look for when you're shopping for a sailboat. It will make you a more educated consumer, and could save you from some unpleasant surprises down the road. Take this book and checklist along on your shopping expeditions as you make what will undoubtedly be one of the most thrilling purchases of your life.

Chapter 1
Deciding What to Buy

Usually the determining factor between buying a new boat or a used one is the cost. Like automobiles, a new boat costs considerably more than an older model due to ever-increasing labor and material costs. If you are careful and do your research, you can get better value per foot of boat by buying a used vessel, and learn far more about your purchase.

One of the first things you have to decide on is the **size** of your boat. This is often determined by:

• The use of the vessel; i.e., weekend or occasional sailing vs. world cruising;

• The number of people you want to carry;

• Whether you're sailing protected waters or offshore;

• The amount of privacy required;

• Affordability (purchase and maintenance).

The next thing you should consider is the **material** used in the construction of the boat. Factors might be:

• The amount of maintenance required;
• Difficulty and cost of possible repairs (would it require professionals?);

• The age of the vessel;
• The sailboat's re-sale value.

At this point, you should consider the **type** of boat that appeals to you. In the end, the boat you buy is often a matter of personal choice.

Boat Design

<u>Heavy displacement</u> - usually has a long keel, tracks well, tends to be slow, has a comfortable motion, but is wetter on deck.

<u>Light displacement</u> - probably a fin keel, more draught, very responsive, usually faster but "bouncier," drier on deck.

<u>Newer designs</u> - tend to be wide, especially aft, having more space below, often an "open" concept. This could be awkward in rough seas if there is a lack of, or inadequate, handholds.

<u>Older designs</u> tend to be narrower, have a more traditional look below and less space.

There are several types of <u>transoms</u>—wide, canoe, double-ended (pointed)—and which can have different angles of slope, even reversed!

<u>Bows</u> can also be different—you may choose a bowsprit which enables you to carry more sail for the length of the hull.

The "pure" sailor may choose an open cockpit for steering to give the sensation of being part of the elements. If it's comfort you desire, you may want to consider a wheel or pilothouse. If you do not want to be dependent on the wind and want to arrive at your destination according to a time schedule, you would probably want a motor sailer—a boat with an engine large enough to carry you at hull speed, no matter what the weather.

For those who do not like to heel over and want a lot of space and privacy, a multi-hull may be the answer. For hull length, the bridge deck catamaran (2 hulls) tends to have more living space than a trimaran (3 hulls). They all have shallow draught and can be beached.

Rigging/Sail Plan

Before deciding what boat to look at, you should think about the type of **sail rig** you want on your vessel. The most common are:

- <u>sloop</u> - 1 foresail and 1 mainsail;
- <u>cutter</u> - 2 foresails and 1 mainsail; or
- <u>ketch</u> - 2 masts, main and mizzen behind, can be rigged like a sloop or a cutter

Cruising catamaran Ara I

Others you might run into are:

- <u>yawl</u> - like the ketch, but the mizzen is stepped behind the rudder post;
- <u>schooner</u> - 2 or more masts with the main being taller than the foremast.

All the above could have a:

- <u>gaff rig</u> - a square sail with a yard on top. This allows a larger sail with a short mast;
- <u>Bermuda rig</u> - a triangle-shaped sail, most common today;
- <u>junk rig</u> - 2 or 3 masts using lug sails;
- <u>free-standing rig</u>– unsupported mast(s), no standing rigging.

*Becoming more common is **roller furling**. This is a means of rolling up the sail, either foresail(s) or the main. It makes putting up sails much easier, especially when sailing short handed. Other <u>advantages</u> are an infinite number of furling combinations, and it can usually be done from the cockpit. <u>Disadvantages</u> are some increased sail chafe, possibility of stretching the sail out of shape and, if fouled, more difficult to fix.*

The final item to look at before deciding on your type of boat is what **limitations** exist. This is somewhat dependent on the use of your vessel:

- Can you do everything that is necessary to physically operate a sailboat of the size you are considering or, would you need a crew?

- Have you taken enough basic courses in navigation, boat handling and safety procedures to operate this vessel?

- If there are two-way radios aboard, are there any licensing requirements?

- Are you considering chartering or using your boat to carry passengers (for hire), and have you looked at what is necessary for your vessel to pass any certification that may be required?

- Can you really afford to buy a boat?

Discussion

Most boat buyers purchase a vessel because they "like the look of her" and forget many of the practical aspects of a sailboat. Some like a clean, simple, streamlined look, while others want a "traditional" vessel with lots of ropes, blocks and wood. (The heavier the better!)

Like many major purchases, boats tend to be an extension of the buyer, a reflection of his or her personality. There is nothing wrong with that, but keep the use of the vessel in mind. If you plan to "gunkhole" (exploring the coves, bays, and other interesting spots along the coast at a leisurely pace), you do not want a boat with a deep draught, or one that is difficult to maneuver and will take up a whole bay to anchor. For single-hand or short-handed sailing, a simple rig like a sloop is more logical than a top-sail schooner. If she is a large vessel, a number of smaller sails like a cutter or ketch rig would be easier to operate than one large sail.

Unless you want a boat to sit at a moorage or dock "for looks," before deciding on a vessel, ask yourself: **"In addition to how pretty she is, can I operate her in the waters I want to sail in, and maintain her within safety standards that are acceptable to me and other boaters?"**

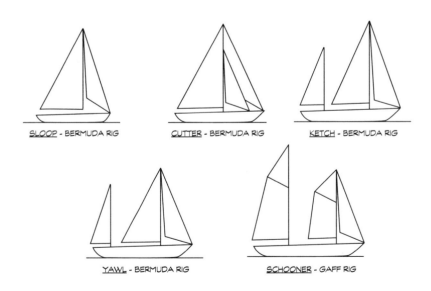

SLOOP - BERMUDA RIG   CUTTER - BERMUDA RIG   KETCH - BERMUDA RIG

YAWL - BERMUDA RIG   SCHOONER - GAFF RIG

11

Chapter 2
Looking at the Boat

One of the most important factors when buying a boat is your initial reaction, the overall look and feel you get. Is the boat:

- Clean and well-maintained (check the hard-to-reach areas, bilges, lockers, etc., look for mildew and water stains).

- Warm and cozy (in other words, could you live on her for extended periods).

- Fresh smelling or is there an unpleasant odor? (This can be very important. Musty and moldy smell can indicate dry rot or, at least, poor ventilation. An acrid smoky smell could be electrical faults, or engine exhaust leaks. A strong fuel smell could be leaking tanks or lines.)

- Wet anywhere? Feel the carpeting (if any) to see if it's wet and also check any fabric wall or head liners. Moisture can indicate leaking windows (or worse), or condensation due to lack of or poor insulation. There is enough water outside the boat!

If possible, meet the former owner(s) of the vessel. You can often tell how the boat was treated by the way the owner talks about her. Why is the owner selling and how much is known about the boat?

*Find out as much **history** as possible:*

- Where was the boat built;

- Former owners;

- Journeys completed;

- Any accidents and damage;

- Look at the logbook, maintenance or repair journals. Are there any systems operation manuals?

- Are there any liens on the vessel, or more than one owner? If the boat is a registered vessel, she will have a book or other papers showing any encumbrances. If not, check a bill-of-sale or any builder certificates. Remember, if you are financing the vessel, the lending institution will look for this information and usually charge you for doing so.

If you are using a broker ask him/her how long the boat has been for sale and if there have been any surveys conducted on the boat. Find out also what is included in the sale—equipment, furnishings, manuals, and any warranties. *Is what you see, what you get?* There have been many occasions when new owners, looking at their purchase, have found items missing, i.e., TV, stereo, which were present on the vessel when previously viewed.

A schooner-rigged classic

If, after your initial positive reaction on seeing the vessel, you feel she is less than perfect because of some of the items mentioned in this section, don't be discouraged yet. Moisture, odors and stains are only indications of problems that may be easily corrected. The important thing is to find the cause, then determine the feasibility and cost of remedying it. Vents can be installed, window seals, hoses and wiring can be replaced. However, rebuilding the sole, bulkheads or cabin top because of deteriorated structural members may be more work than you want to do.

Chapter 3
Looking at the Hull

A dictionary definition of a "hull" states that the word comes from the German "Hulla," which means a cloak or covering. It refers to the main body of a boat, bottom, sides and upper deck -- not including masts, rigging, fittings and engines. For the purpose of this guide, the hull and deck are treated separately, the latter including the structures on the deck.

Hulls come in various shapes, some dependent on the material used while others are designed for specific purposes. To go into the finer points of hull design would fill several books and is outside the scope of this guide. You can, however, walk around a marina and ask boat owners how they like their craft. Ask about the positive and negative aspects of the different styles.

There are two broad categories used frequently by boaters: the **displacement** hull and the **planing** hull. The former usually alludes to a sailing vessel, probably older in design, while the latter refers to either a motorboat or a newer design racing sailboat. In actual fact the two categories mean totally different characteristics of hull design. Displacement is the amount of water a boat displaces being fully loaded with water and fuel. This can therefore refer to a "displacement hull" or a "planing hull."

Planing is the action of a hull while moving through water and depends on the weight, shape and propulsion of the vessel. For a boat to plane, it has to lift to the surface of the water. A primary element of hull design is that the waterline length (the distance between the bow wave and the stern wave), limits the speed of a vessel. (For those technically inclined, this "hull speed" is calculated as 1.34 x the square root of the length of the boat's waterline.) To go faster than this, a boat must lift itself out of the water and climb up and partially over the bow wave. This is possible by having a lot of power or, more frequently, a light-weight design with a flat bottom.

With the newer, faster sailboats, one can see a fine entry with the hull flattening and widening towards the stern. Under the right wind conditions, these vessels would plane, doubling their hull speed. However the drawback of a flat bottom is that the vessel can pound severely in rough seas -- very uncomfortable for the crew! A displacement hull will tend to cut through the waves, giving a more comfortable ride.

When choosing a hull shape, one has to consider what you are going to use the boat for. A full keel and rounded hull will slip through the water easily and track well. A fin keel with a rounded hull will be more responsive in the turns but can be more difficult to keep on track. A compromise is a fixed (molded as part of the hull) keel with a cutaway forefoot. All of these would fall under the waterline speed limitation. One could flatten the hull aft, giving a little more rise at speed, a semi-planing hull. Hard chine construction is simpler to build and gives a stiffer heeling angle initially than a round bottom, but is usually slower in acceleration. A flat or half-round bow section will tend to pound into the waves, but will give a drier deck, while one with a sharp V section will cut through the waves but will throw the water up and over the deck.

As you can see, there are many variables involved in choosing a hull!

HULL CONSTRUCTION
■ **Wood**— There are four main wooden boat building methods:

Plywood uses sheets of wood laminations (various thickness) cut from patterns and fastened to frames. A variation of this is using strips of veneer and, by diagonal, vertical and horizontal layering, glue them together to form a monocoque structure. The wood is then painted, varnished or covered with combinations of epoxy or polyester resins and fiberglass. *Advantages are the boat's light weight and strength.*

Carvel Planked are wooden planks running fore and aft fastened to wooden frames and flush fitted to one another to form a smooth surface. The seams are usually caulked with cotton and a sealing compound to make it waterproof. *Advantages are long life (in wood building) and ease of repair.*

Lapstrake are overlapping wooden boards running fore and aft, fastened to one another and to wood frames. *Advantages are great strength, but it is difficult to repair leaks.*

<u>Strip Planked</u> use squarish strips of wood edge-nailed and/or glued to one another over fewer or no frames, giving a smooth monocoque hull. It is usually covered with fiberglass or something similar, encapsulating the wood. *Advantages are high strength, but difficult to repair.*

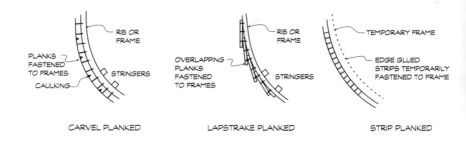

TYPICAL WOOD HULL CONSTRUCTION

When examining any wooden hull, look for:

- <u>Soft spots</u> - dry rot, electrolysis, collision damage;

- <u>Delamination</u> of wood layers, or wood/glass layers (can often be checked by tapping hull and listening to the difference in sound);

- <u>Fastenings</u> (if any used) - discoloration of wood usually indicates some sort of fastener disintegration due to electrolysis or oxidation.

Discussion

In general terms, wood is still the traditional method of boat construction and sailing vessels made out of wood are usually "traditional" in design; i.e., full keel, heavy displacement, and narrow. The exceptions are those built out of wood/epoxy laminates, giving the boat a high-strength, light, monocoque structure. These are generally fast-cruising or racing boats.

Traditional wood construction still has a romantic quality not found in other building methods. However, there is a high level of maintenance necessary and careful inspection is required when purchasing a wooden boat. Dry rot is one of the biggest problems found in older vessels. The area affected is soft, punky, and disintegrates when examined. It is caused by fungi that develop in poorly ventilated areas. It can spread quickly and, if found, usually means repairing or replacing quite a large area. There are epoxy-based stabilizers on the market that kill the fungi spores and "plasticize" the wood, returning some of its previous strength. (This is not recommended for structural members or large infected areas.)

Wood delaminations can sometimes be repaired by injecting epoxy through small holes drilled between the layers and temporarily fastening them until the epoxy is cured. A similar process can be used with GRP delaminations, especially if it is localized damage and not due to a resin-poor lay-up. Needless to say, soft spots and delaminations can be costly to repair.

■ Fiberglass/Glass Reinforced Plastic (GRP) Hulls

This type of hull uses glass fibers either random, woven or stacked, laid-up or blown, in combination with a binder, usually polyester resin inside or over a mold. There are a number of types of polyester resin including fire-resistant ones. Other resins include a variety of epoxies and vinyls. All have different properties in strength and flexibility. Hull finish is usually a pigmented resin (gelcoat) or is painted with various paints—the best being a two-part linear polyurethane. GRP or fiberglass boats can be solid construction, have a foam, wood or honeycomb core for less weight, or be a combination of all. *Advantages of GRP are reduced maintenance, resistance to deterioration, and monocoque structure.*

When checking a hull, look for:

• Cracks (don't confuse small cracks or crazing in the gelcoat for structural cracks) - caused by stress or collision;

• Blisters - water-filled bubbles due to osmosis. (If they are less than 1/8" in size and few in number, they can be easily repaired with epoxy fillers);

• Delamination - can be glass fiber or core delamination caused by collision, hard use, or resin-poor lay-up.

Discussion

One of the more controversial problems in fiberglass (GRP) vessels is the presence of blisters (due to osmosis) on the hull. Some marine experts advocate removing the entire outer gelcoat layer under the water line by grinding or planing with a special tool, drying out the glass fiber and re-surfacing the hull with an epoxy-based compound. This is a very expensive procedure. Whether this is a structural necessity or merely cosmetic is arguable. It is true that moisture in the glass fibers add weight to the vessel, however, it is generally not enough to make a difference in boat performance unless she is a weight-sensitive racing vessel. It is highly doubtful that if the hull is heavy and has a solid GRP lay-up (or, if cored, has a thick outer layer), there would be any significant reduction in hull strength. There would be a problem if the original GRP lay-up was resin poor, where water entry could cause a thickening of the glass fibers leading to delamination. If you suspect the latter, it would be wise to drill out a small plug sample, or grind out one of the blisters and check the GRP composition.

■ Steel Hulls

All steel boats today are of welded construction. Various types of steel can be used, including some that are rust resistant. Plates are cut from patterns and either used flat in hard chine construction, or rolled for round bilge construction. Plates are usually welded to frames with longitudinal stringers, although there are methods using few or no frames, relying on the rigidity of the material for strength. *Advantages are strength, easy construction, and relatively inexpensive materials— in small vessels, weight can be a problem.*

Main things to look out for in welds:

- Stress cracks;

- Corrosion - poor penetration, wrong welding rods (dirty welds);

- Excessive grinding - poor penetration;

- Uneven plating due to faulty sequencing of welds;

Other things to consider:

• Excessive corrosion or pitting caused by improper paint preparation or electrolysis from combination of unsuitable materials;

• Excessive application of fairing compounds to cover up errors in construction (they eventually lift off from steel due to corrosion, vibration, collisions).

The 55' steel, round-bilged ketch Northanger

■ Aluminum Hulls

Aluminum construction is similar to steel construction, although the welds are not as strong as the parent material and require more skill to do. Attention to welds is very important. *Advantages are light material that is very easy to cut, and reduced maintenance due to corrosion resistance.*

Check for:
• Thorough penetration of welds and evenness of runs;

• The grade of aluminum used (especially if not professionally built—cheaper but not corrosion-resistant alloys are often used);

- Electrolysis or pitting - if non-compatible materials are used (or not insulated) such as bronze, severe deterioration can occur;

- Corrosion - could be due to application of unsuitable paint;

- Stress cracks, especially at welds.

Discussion

When viewing a steel or aluminum hull and corrosion is present (often on the inside), check the amount. In other words, how much parent metal is remaining? With heavier plating, a 15-20% reduction is tolerable as long as continued corrosion is checked. In cases of severe pitting, there is usually something else happening than just oxidation, for example, electrolysis. The cause should be carefully checked out and, if pitting is severe enough (50% or more), re-plating will be necessary.

Weld penetration, especially on aluminum hulls, is critical. Corrosion around a weld could indicate inadequate bonding of metals due to low heat (amperage), incorrect electrodes, poor penetration, or pollution by foreign matter. Beware of welds that show signs of heavy grinding, this could indicate surface welds with very little penetration.

■ Ferro-cement Hulls

These hulls utilize a rich mortar mixture reinforced with an armature of thin steel rods and mesh built in or usually on the outside of a mold. The cement can be plastered or sprayed on the steel. Proper curing of the product is critical. The main problem with purchasing a ferro-cement boat is the difficulty (except if X-rayed) in determining the penetration of the mortar and the condition or amount of steel reinforcement. *Advantages are strength and durability, inexpensive materials and ease of repair, but weight can be a problem in small vessels.*

Steel armature of a ferro-cement yacht

Check for:

- <u>Cracks</u> – It is often difficult to tell if it's a surface crack or a structural fault;

- <u>Discoloration</u> - If the crack goes into the steel reinforcement, there will be corrosion visible;

- <u>Improper curing</u> - If properly cured, surface will be very hard and tapping on the hull will produce a "ringing" tone; a bad cure produces a "dead" sound;

- <u>Blisters</u>- in the paint finish usually indicate the surface has not been properly prepared, cured, or there is water entry, probably from the inside;

- <u>Thickness</u> - There is an optimal relationship between the amount of steel, length of vessel and thickness of hull (usually not more than 3/16" of cement over the steel inside and out). Thicker does not necessarily mean stronger; it only adds more weight.

Discussion

Ferro-cement hulls are more difficult to check, which is probably why they often sell far below their value. A poorly constructed hull may look fine from the outside, but will eventually cause severe problems. It helps if the boat has a complete construction record available, with photos, curing charts, etc. Otherwise, it is recommended to remove some of the through-hull fittings, or drill a core out of the hull to check the reinforcing and cement composition. Many ferro-cement boats built commercially (often using split steel molds, pressure application methods, and rigid material specifications) are as good as boats built from any other material.

A well-finished ferro-cement boat looks just like any other boat—beautiful!

Chapter 4
Looking at the Deck

The same information, advantages and suggestions found in Chapter 3 (Looking at the Hull) apply for the deck and cabin structures. The only significant difference is that the deck has greater exposure to the deteriorating effects of sunlight; i.e., ultraviolet radiation (UV). You must expect to see more fading or oxidation of GRP. Varnishes and other clear coatings over wood always deteriorate faster with UV exposure. The abrasive effects of rain, dust and snow will rust the most carefully prepared steel and aluminum. The important thing to evaluate is the <u>extent</u> of the deterioration.

When you first look at the deck, check the **layout.**

- What is the visibility from the steering position, on the deck and around the boat?

- Are winches, rope clutches, and other sailing hardware accessible and of sufficient number and size?
- If there is an open cockpit, is there any weather protection?

- If a wheelhouse is present, is it possible to sail the boat from there?

- Is there seating available for captain/crew, and are there storage lockers?

What is the condition of:

- Anti-skid proofing. Is there some on the deck and cabin tops?

- The railings/lifelines. Are they of sufficient height and strength to keep you on deck?

- The deck fittings. Are they caulked and secure?

- Hatches and doors. They should be weathertight with adequate closing devices. If they are transparent what is the material—safety glass, reinforced glass, polycarbonate [Lexan] or Plexiglas? (The latter two will deteriorate over time and get brittle from UV radiation.)

Carefully check:

- <u>Running rigging</u> (see glossary)- Is it the proper size? Is it frayed, worn or deteriorated from UV (hard, prickly)?

- <u>Standing rigging</u> (see glossary)- Is it stainless or galvanized steel? How old is it? Is there any discoloration at swaged or clamped ends (corrosion)? Are turnbuckles seized or free and do they have locking pins? What is the tension? (If loose, could indicate excessive stretch from stress.)

The deck of Toolka II, *a fiberglass cutter*

- <u>Sails</u> - What is the material and weight? Are there any reef points? How old? Are there any ripped seams or excessive wear? Baggy (over-stretched)? How many sails?

- <u>Mast(s) and boom(s)</u> - What material is it made of? Condition? (If aluminum, any corrosion; if wood, any cracks, dry rot). Is it weather-proofed (anodized, lacquered, painted)? What is the condition of tangs and other fittings (cracks, worn holes or pins, if aluminum, do the holes have stainless steel inserts?)

Do the sheaves or blocks turn freely? Is there any wear? Is the mast stepped on deck (check corrosion at step) or on keel? (Check mastboot for leaks). Is there access to top of mast (steps, bosun's chair)? Is there access to mast wiring? Are there any pull wires to put in additional circuits? Any sound insulation? If there is roller furling, does it rotate freely and when was it last serviced? Are there any other poles; i.e., spinnaker pole?

When the "checks" become very important

If there is an **anchor winch** on the vessel:

- <u>Manual</u> – Is the winch an adequate size for the anchor? Is the handle accessible?

- <u>Electric</u> – Check the condition of the motor. Is the amperage draw appropriate for the wiring and battery size? Is there any corrosion from deck leaks or condensation?

- <u>Hydraulic</u> – Are there fluid leaks? Does the hydraulic system require the main engine to operate or does it run on its own power pack?

Anchors:

Check for:

- Number, type and condition.

- How many, what type and how stored?

- Verify the amount and size of chain and anchor rode.

- Is the anchor adequate for the bottom conditions you will be encountering?

- Check the condition of shackles, and if pins are secured.

- Is the "bitter end" secured?

- If a chain locker, is there a drain?

Any other deck hardware:

- Sail track - (genoa or stay sail sheeting) Check condition of cars. Is track secure?

- Bow roller(s) - Check pin(s).

- Bow sprit - Check if secure.

- Grab rails – Check for condition, sufficient number and if they are securely fastened.

- Sheet and halyard winches – Check for condition and wear, any grinding noises or a loose drum (bearings gone). Base should be securely fastened. When were they last serviced?

Discussion

A word about anchors, grab rails and lifelines.

■ There is no single anchor that is good in all conditions, although many manufacturers will claim theirs is. Some work extremely well in sand or mud, others in rock. With the former, remember that often, to get to the sand or mud, you may have to penetrate a pretty dense ground cover such as eel grass or kelp. So, get an anchor with some weight behind it to get through this foliage. A fisherman or stocked anchor, although very awkward, is still the best to use with rocky bottoms— all those ends will eventually hook onto something. Also, unless you are young, strong, or foolish, consider an anchor winch. Pulling up a 60-lb. anchor, a 100-ft. or so of chain, plus breaking it out of the mud by hand, can be very daunting.

■ A boat can never have enough grab rails. In rough or confused seas, there is nothing worse than facing a heaving expanse of deck with nothing to hang on to. When viewing the deck of a vessel, check that no matter where you are, there is at least one handhold. Check the railings and make sure they are comfortable to grip; don't necessarily go for looks—ease of use and strength are more important.

■ Lifelines fall into the same category as grabrails, although they surround the deck of a boat. The safest ones are still the solid variety, which you almost never see except in very large vessels. Reaching for a solid bit of pipe or wood is far more reassuring than a line or cable that moves around. Unfortunately, most sailboats you will see have vinyl-covered, stainless steel cable or a plastic fiber material. Check its breaking strength, with a safety margin of at least 3 to 1. Check the ends and the tightness. For some strange reason, many boats have very loose lifelines—not the most comforting thought when your life may depend on it!

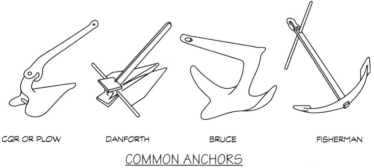

| CQR OR PLOW | DANFORTH | BRUCE | FISHERMAN |

COMMON ANCHORS

As mentioned at the beginning of this section, many items discussed in Chapter 3 (Looking at the Hull) apply to decks as well. However, often the structural makeup is different from the hull. This is especially so in "cored" boats. For example, many boat builders will use a balsa wood core above the waterline but not below; the reasoning is that minor damage might allow water to seep into the wood core causing deterioration. If the coring is properly done, each separate piece of end grain wood has a slight gap to the next piece allowing it to be surrounded by resin. Thus, any water entry would be restricted to the damaged piece. Improper coring would allow the deterioration to spread.

You might ask why use wood at all, since there are a variety of inert foam cores available that would not be affected by any water penetration. It has been found, especially in older vessels, that wood core hulls do not delaminate as often as foam core hulls. This could be due to a better mechanical adherence to wood, especially if it is encapsulated. Delamination could be caused by collision, repeated pounding into waves, or even excessive vibration from the engine. In later years, builders started using small squares of foam, copying the encapsulation principle of balsa core, or grooving the foam sheets to give them more "holding power" by providing keyways to the resin.

Decks (and deck structures) are more susceptible to weathering than hulls. Sunlight, or ultraviolet radiation, is especially hard on wood. It must be remembered that wood with a clear surface preparation, whether it is varnish, epoxy, or whatever, will break down quite quickly with sun exposure. The only way to prevent this is using a completely opaque cover such as paint, preferably a color that reflects rather than absorbs. Heat can cause over-expansion and contraction resulting in cracks which, in turn, could allow water entry. Moisture has a way of penetrating between layers and getting trapped, resulting in eventual deterioration. To some extent, the same can happen with steel or aluminum vessels; expansion and contraction from heating and cooling can form small cracks especially around welds, or any connections of dissimilar materials.

GRP surfaces oxidize or fade over time from UV radiation. Fortunately, with a little work and any number of mild abrasive/wax compounds, the surface can look as good as new. This, of course, depends on the thickness of the outer gelcoat layer, since oxidation and the abrasives will take off a small amount of the surface.

Polypropylene-based ropes are also affected by UV radiation, where fibers deteriorate and become brittle. A simple method of checking is to feel the rope.

One weathering effect that is becoming more prevalent is surface deterioration due to contaminants in the air. The most common one is "acid rain." This can attack not only steel and aluminum vessels, but also wooden and GRP boats. The least damaging result is bad staining but, it can also cause pitting, blistering, and breakdown in wood fibers. Even vinyl and other soft plastics are affected. Look closely at plastic Dorade vents, for example.

The standing rigging on a boat is often taken for granted, more so than the condition of the engine, even though the former is supposed to be the primary method of propulsion. In the "old days" it was much easier to check and, if it looked rusty, replace it! Some sailors still prefer using galvanized-standing rigging for that reason. Stainless wire always "looks new" even though there can be hairline fractures due to metal fatigue or vibration, not apparent to the naked eye. Generally, if the vessel has been used, and if the stainless rigging is over 10 years old, think about replacement. The time period is less in hotter climates. At least look at the rigging more carefully, especially around the turn buckles or end fittings. Discoloration, thickening or thinning of strands, or using a dye may indicate fractures or other metal stress.

Deck fastenings are also worthy of more attention. Cleats, tracks, railings, and eyes, may look in good condition, however, if the screws or bolts fail, the result could be disastrous as well as expensive. It is amazing how many vessels have loose deck hardware. In wooden vessels rot often occurs under deck mounts. There might also be an acidic reaction on the fastenings themselves causing a deterioration that is invisible until you remove them for inspection.

In GRP decks, insufficient backing plates or washers could lead to wear that loosens bolts. The fibers could become over-compressed, also loosening the piece of hardware, which in turn, may expand the fastening holes by vibration or movement, leading to eventual failure of the fastening. The same thing could occur in ferro-cement vessels. In steel or aluminum boats, corrosion of the deck or the fastening due to poor caulking, or poor welding is usually the cause of deck hardware problems. If you suspect this, it is worth removing some of the fastenings or mounts at random to check their condition.

Chapter 5
Looking at the Interior

The interior layout is as -- if not more -- important than the deck layout. This is the sailors' hideaway when things get nasty outside. It is also where you relax, sleep, cook, and possibly entertain. As mentioned at the beginning of this guide, *it is often the first look that decides whether this boat is for you.*

There are many types of interiors, from those made of almost maintenance-free fiberglass or other plastics, to wooden finishes or a combination of both. What you buy boils down to personal preference. What is important is accessibility—access to the galley, head, cabins, engine, storage, etc.

A view of a galley layout

Galley

Things to check:

- Is the <u>arrangement</u> suitable? Is there access to adequate fresh air (vent, hatch, or porthole)? Is there enough light?

- <u>Stove</u> - Is it large enough? Is there an oven? What is the fuel?

What are the safety guards (gimbals, railings around burners, sensors, fireproofing, access to an extinguisher, brace in case of rough weather)?

- Refrigeration, (or cool chest)- Check the power source; if it's electric how much does it draw? When was the coolant last checked? *(Propane-operated fridges are generally a "no," especially on a sailboat, because of the open flame and need for a level surface to operate properly.)*

- Dishes – How are they to be stored and how easy is the access?

- Sinks and drains - Is the plumbing sound? Are the lines of adequate size? *(Two small deep sinks are better than one large sink for water usage.)*

- Pump - Is the fresh water pump manual or electric? When was it last serviced? If it's an offshore sailboat, does it have a salt water pump in the galley to conserve fresh water?

Discussion

When talking to sailors, every one has at least one tale to tell about flying bodies and broken tables (or bones) in rough weather. The stories get worse when you mention galleys and cooking. It is most important that the "cook" can perform his or her duties with both hands available. This means some sort of bracing system, or sling, unless they can cook and juggle at the same time!

Usually the limited size of a boat also restricts the size of the galley, so that it is possible to perform one's duties without careening from one side to the other. Tight cupboard doors with catches, dish and cup racks that keep the dishes in place, guards around the stove, stove gimbals (unless a multi-hull), drawers with catches, are all requirements on a boat. Top-loading storage areas, although they may be more difficult to access, will keep stuff in place when looking for an item. If you want to stay simple with manual water pumps, consider a foot pump to keep both hands free.

Head

The head is often the most neglected place on a boat, and yet is one of the most important since this is where usually the largest through hull fitting under the water line is located.

Check the following carefully (giving special attention to hose clamps).

- Is there a manual or electric toilet?

- Does the pump feel sloppy or worn?

- When was it serviced last? Were the hoses checked for calcium build-up?

- Is there easy access to shutoff?

- Is there a holding tank or other waste disposal system; i.e., Lectro San? Does it comply with local requirements?

- Are there any visible leaks or is there a smell around the toilet? (If there is, it usually means a leak or lack of servicing.)

- Are there any shower facilities (where applicable)? Where do they drain? (The shower should have its own drain tank or pump.)

- Is there a sink and storage lockers?

- Is there adequate ventilation?

Left, a comfortable head, with shower and bath (holding tank behind)

Right, sleeping cabin on a 42-foot cruising catamaran

Discussion

Although the basic requirements as to space, storage, etc., for galleys can be applied to the ship's head, one item that is different, but most important, is the toilet itself. There are many makes and models, but generally marine toilets fall into three categories. There is the manual pumped one using a diaphragm set up at the bottom of the bowl, another using a manual piston pump usually on the side, and the electric toilet using a motor-driven pump.

Invariably, sometime, somewhere, the toilet will stop functioning (it's usually plugged) and will have to be removed, cleaned, or rebuilt. Because of space limitations, most boat toilets are a nightmare to remove. Bolts are virtually inaccessible and probably corroded. To get at them often means getting on your knees, stomach or upside down in extreme cases. Since there is a problem, waste is usually still present in the system somewhere. If you are lucky, the vessel is at a dock or anchorage. If it's not, the additional movement only increases an already unpleasant situation. When you look at a boat's head, keep all this in mind, and check accessibility and ease of removal very carefully. I have seen vessels with 2 or 3 heads, all not functioning, because no one knew how to remove them, or couldn't.

Holding tanks are becoming a must in many areas. When viewing an older vessel with a tank, check for smell. Many have been put in improperly after the vessel was built and it may be a considerable job and expense to change. If the boat does not have a tank, see if there is space for one or consider another method of waste disposal.

Sometimes showers are drained into the main bilge and then pumped out. The reasoning behind this is that the soapy shower water will keep the bilge clean. Unfortunately, the opposite is true. Soap can coagulate with oil residue, causing an unseemly and smelly mess that is not easily removed.

Berths and cabins

Often, one of the "selling" points of a boat is that it "can sleep eight" (or more). The buyer needs to ask whether he/she really wants to sleep eight and, if so, eight what—adults, children…? In many cases, accommodations are less than comfortable.

Check:

- The size (length and width) of berths.

- What type, thickness and condition of bedding (foam or canvas)?

- The location of berths. Are they fixed, convertible, in the salon, or in a separate cabin?

- Is the privacy adequate for your needs?

When travelling in rough seas, remember the most comfortable place is at the center axis of the vessel, not up front where most sleeping areas are located.

- Check on the amount of <u>dry</u> storage under and above the berths. More is better.

Main salon on a 42-foot cruising catamaran

Discussion

When looking at the accommodation available in a vessel, consider your immediate needs. If there are only two of you most of the time using this vessel, buy something with berths for two. Probably, there will be space available on the settees, or convertible table, or

34

even the cockpit, for those times you may have guests. Too many boat buyers purchase something that will sleep eight, and never use the extra space. All it means is additional expense and maintenance.

The thing buyers most often forget when viewing a vessel at a dock or on land, is that it is meant to move, and not always only in a forward direction. It is one of the most difficult concepts for a boating novice to accept, that this seemingly solid platform can move up and down as well as sideways, all at once in the right conditions. Water is a fluid medium, and is very seldom flat and calm. It is affected by winds, tides, currents—you name it—and, sometimes, all these together. When you look at a boat's interior, remember this. It is nice to have a lot of clear space, but not when that space moves around. There must be places you can brace yourself, or holds on which to grab.

Engine room or compartment

In sailboats, engines tend to be placed in out-of-the-way or difficult-to-reach areas, since they are thought of as auxiliary only. This "out-of-sight, out-of-mind" approach can often lead to forgotten maintenance. In Chapter 6 we will be looking at engines in more detail.

At this point, check:

• Accessibility to *all* parts of the engine, especially the areas that require regular maintenance; i.e., belts, filters, oil fill, etc.

• If the engine compartment is soundproofed and fireproofed?

• If there is enough ventilation (which can be shut off in case of fire)?

Chapter 6
Looking at the Engine

In a sailboat, the engine is regarded as auxiliary power and the sails as primary power. A motor sailer regards sails and engine equally. The question a buyer often asks is: how big (amount of horsepower) should my auxiliary engine be? Although this is a matter of personal preference, it depends a great deal on the vessel. *The engine should have sufficient power; i.e., when being driven onto a lee shore it should have enough power to propel the vessel to safety without sails in reasonable circumstances.*

Auxiliary power for sailboats fall into two categories: **inboards** and **outboards**. For those who know very little about boat engines, an inboard is exactly that, an engine that is placed somewhere inside the vessel. It usually has external fuel tanks, and various types of transmissions and drives. The outboard is a self-contained motor, normally hung off the transom or in a designated well in the aft part of the boat. It can have a built-in or separate fuel tank The transmission/drive is normally an integral part of the engine, and it usually runs on gasoline (although diesel outboards are becoming more popular). Outboard motors can be 2 cycle (oil added to the gasoline) or 4 cycle and usually have an extra-long shaft because of the transom height of a sailboat.

Even though most engines, inboard and outboard, have electric starters, some still have a capability to manual start using a handle or cord. There are others that have several choices for starting, i.e., compressed air, or using the expanding gasses of an explosive shell.

The construction and condition of engine bearers and mounting bolts are all important, since not only do they have to support the weight of the engine, but also absorb the vibration and thrust that the engine produces. In the case of outboard motors, most sailboat transoms have to be reinforced. One must also remember the violent movements a vessel can produce in rough weather conditions (the boat could even turn upside down). The resulting torque, if not properly secured, could easily rip an engine from its mountings, or bearers from the hull or bulkheads.

When examining a boat engine, check on:

- Type, size and age (number of running hours);

- Accessibility and cost of spare parts;

- Type of cooling (air, water - fresh or salt). Does it use a heat exchanger or have exterior cooling?;

- If using salt water, pump and a heat exchanger, is there a raw water filter?;

- When were the engine zinc anodes replaced?;

- Are there any obvious oil or water leaks (check bilge);

- Are the belts worn? Tight? Are they the correct size, especially width and angle of V?;

- The condition of hoses and clamps;

- Whether the mounts are secure;

- The type and condition of exhaust system, wet or dry? (Examine hoses for leaks, mufflers for cracks, clamps for deterioration.);

- Whether the fuel lines copper or flame-resistant? Check connections for leaks;

- The number and type of fuel filters. Is there a water trap?

 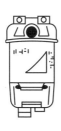  

Examples of fuel filters

If it's a gasoline engine, is there a:

• Flame arrester on the carburetor? Blower? Fuel vapor sensor?

If it's a diesel engine:

• When have the injectors been checked or overhauled?

• Is there oil in the injector fuel pump? (Most injector pumps have a small oil sump for lubricating the moving parts. There is a small dipstick for checking. Over time the oil tends to get diluted with minute amounts of diesel fuel that bypasses the pistons in the pump, so to all appearances the sump is full. However, make sure it is oil, not an oil/fuel mix. The latter does not lubricate as well.)

Discussion

With the availability of the modern, light and efficient outboard motor, one doesn't see many inboard gasoline engines in new sailing vessels. Even some of the larger boats use gasoline outboards. However, one still runs across the occasional "Atomic 4" or similar, in older sailboats. There are decided advantages to gasoline engines. They are generally lighter, easier to work on, cleaner, definitely cheaper to buy and to maintain and—for those inclined to motion sickness—the exhaust is not quite as nausea-inducing as that of diesel smoke.

Of course, there are disadvantages, the main one being the volatility of gasoline. Insurance companies usually get very nervous with inboard gasoline-powered boats. Outboard engines with outboard tanks, are more in favor. If one has a properly installed engine that is well maintained with all the various safety gear installed (blowers, gas sniffers, flame arresters, and so forth) the chances of a mishap are minimal.

With larger vessels or serious cruising boats, a diesel engine is definitely the engine of choice. Their increased weight also means more durability. Diesel fuel is readily accessible internationally, especially in the more isolated areas. There is no electricity involved in the actual running of the engine, thus eliminating a common source of problems in a marine environment. Additionally, diesel can be used for heating and cooking as well. However, for local boating or coastal cruising don't discount your choice of a sailboat just because it has an inboard gasoline engine.

Cooling the engine has always been a source of discussion among the boating community. Each method has its advantages and disadvantages. The most common is the fresh water-cooled engine with a saltwater-cooled heat exchanger. Basically, the fresh water is pumped by the engine through a series of tubes which are surrounded by saltwater (also pumped by an external pump by the engine). The fresh water is then injected into the exhaust manifold (cooling that) and into the exhaust pipe mixing with the engine exhaust cooling and muffling it and out through a through hull fitting. The advantages are that the engine itself only has fresh water in it, the entire cooling system is inside the vessel (except for the inlet and outlet), the exhaust is cooled, therefore, the exhaust "pipe" can be a flexible hose, and it is reasonably easy to repair. Disadvantages are the possibility of flooding the engine (and the boat) with saltwater siphoning back through the exhaust. Care must be taken to ensure the "exhaust loop" is above the waterline in all circumstances and that it has an anti-siphoning valve. The latter must be checked on a regular basis, since it can plug up with hydrocarbons and salt. The heat exchanger must have sacrificial zincs to prevent the possibility of pinhole leaks developing in the tubes through electrolysis. These zincs are usually replaced annually.

Another option often seen in commercial vessels is exterior cooling tubes along the hull or keel. The fresh water of the engine system is pumped through these tubes with the water outside doing the cooling. Advantages are no additional pump or separate heat exchanger, thus being a simpler system. There is no possibility of siphoning saltwater into the engine, but of course this means no water-cooled exhaust pipe. The tubes on the outside are also more vulnerable to objects hitting them. However, if holed, the engine will still be cooled, although with saltwater which, in an emergency, is better than having no engine.

There are engines on the market that do use saltwater for cooling directly, eliminating the heat exchanger, but retaining the water-cooled exhaust. There are sacrificial zincs in the engine water-jacket to prevent electrolysis. A disadvantage is that whatever is in the saltwater will go through your engine although, as in using a heat exchanger, there is a salt (or raw) water filter installed at the inlet. However, this is mainly for weeds and other coarse material, and will not filter out sand or water contaminants. In all likelihood, a direct cooling system would cause more wear and tear on your engine.

The last type of cooling used is air-cooling. These are usually seen on lighter engines with more surface area and a large fan. The obvious advantage is not to have to worry about water getting into your engine and, of course, fewer pumps. The disadvantages are they do tend to be noisier, run at a higher temperature and take up more room. Of course, the latter could be useful in colder climates and there are excellent soundproofing materials available for engine compartments.

DRIVES/TRANSMISSIONS

The drive takes the power from the engine and through a number of mechanical or hydraulic gears transfers this power, usually in some ratio, i.e., 2:1 or 3:1, to the stern assembly. This can be part of the engine or a completely separate installation. In the latter it is important to note the support system of the propeller shaft. There should be some sort of bearing, i.e., pillow block, or thrust block -- every 6 feet. In sailboats with engines aft this is not a problem. However a 40-foot vessel with the engine located amidships could easily have a 12 feet or more shaft.

Inboard drives include:

SAIL DRIVE - The drive/propeller assembly is attached at 90 degrees to the back of the motor, extending out of the bottom of the boat. *Advantages are: it is usually a complete unit meant for use on sailing vessels. The through hull drive unit is heavily flanged, sealed and fastened to the hull. Disadvantages are: it is not suitable for all boats, i.e. full keel vessels; it is quite expensive to purchase and repair; and the stern assembly is more vulnerable in case of grounding.*

STRAIGHT DRIVE – The propeller shaft assembly is in a straight line from the back of the engine. The entire drive train is usually at a slight angle coming out of the vessel through a stuffing box, a propeller tube and the cutless bearing, behind the keel and in front of the rudder. *Advantages are: it can be used on most hulls; it's usually easier (and cheaper) to repair; it is very adaptable in case of engine/gearbox changes. Disadvantages are: it usually requires* *more maintenance, i.e. stuffing box, flexible couplings, and keeping the engine aligned with the stern gear.*

V DRIVE - The engine is mounted backwards with the drive coming off the back at 180 degrees. (There are variations; some engines have a complicated gear set-up so that they are still mounted forward with the drive coming off the front.) *Advantages are: mainly that it takes up less longitudinal space therefore is more suitable for smaller vessels. Disadvantages are: it is more difficult to repair because of lack of space; and it is more expensive to purchase and maintain.*

HYDRAULIC DRIVE - The engine operates a hydraulic rotary pump which in turn pumps hydraulic oil to a hydraulic motor through high-pressure hoses. *Advantages are: there is no shaft line-up necessary, the engine can be placed anywhere in the vessel; hydraulic motors are generally very small in size and require very little maintenance. It is not directly connected to propeller shaft and is therefore easier on the engine if propeller is grounded or jammed. Disadvantages are: some power loss (5-15%) through power transfer, additional system (hydraulic oil); more expensive to install.*

With transmissions check to see:

- What type (most are hydraulic) and ratio (number of running hours)?

- Can it "free wheel" or be locked while sailing?

- Is there a flexible coupling or thrust bearing? What is the condition?

Propeller Shaft

- What is its size and what material is it made of?

- If there is a grounding strap or brush present? Check wear. (Discoloration of shaft material could indicate heat which may have weakened the shaft.)

- Check the condition of stuffing box. (If metal looks worn, shaft could be out of alignment.) Although most stuffing boxes use a Teflon or similar stuffing compound, other shaft seals include packless sealing systems using nitrite seals, some with oil reservoirs.

- Verify the condition of cutless bearing (calls for an out-of-water inspection).

- Check the size and type of propeller(s), (diameter, pitch, fixed or folding). Are there any spares?

- Inspect the material of propeller(s). (Discoloration or pitting could indicate galvanic corrosion.)

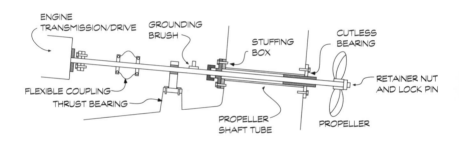

TYPICAL PROPELLER DRIVE ASSEMBLY

Discussion

Propeller shafts and stuffing boxes are also great topics of conversation among boat enthusiasts. This is probably because it is an area also "open" to all that water outside the boat. The stuffing box is what stands in the way of it coming in or not.

There are two basic types—the "drip" and the "dripless." The first allows a very small amount of water to come through the packing, cooling the surface and acting as a lubricant. There are quite a few varieties of packing available, and one must be careful to use one that works with the type of stuffing box and material on the vessel. There have been cases where the stuffing reacted with the water and the metal to score the propeller shaft. With the "drip" type of box, water has to come through otherwise the shaft will get too hot and cause damage.

The "dripless" variety can either be oil seals and nitrite bearings on either end, with an oil reservoir providing the lubrication, or, it can be ball or rollerbearings and seals fixed to the shaft. Many of the "old-timers" don't trust the dripless, feeling that the water is essential for cooling.

When inspecting the shaft assembly, no matter what type, the main thing to look for is heat discoloration in the shaft or bearing and any indication of wear. Since both can be accentuated by shaft vibration or misalignment, look at the condition of the engine mounts. The installation of a flexible coupling can often decrease vibration from small amounts of misalignment, as well as isolate the engine somewhat from the propeller. Many engine crankshafts have broken when the shock of hitting a rock or a log was directly transferred from the propeller through the shaft to the engine. This is especially true when there was a mechanical or direct-drive transmission. Hydraulic transmissions, on the other hand, help dampen shock and provide some protection to the engine.

Chapter 7
Looking at the Sailboat's Systems

In today's world of rapidly changing technology it is easy to go to extremes with systems for boats. Most of these advances are there to make our life easier or simpler; unfortunately, often the opposite happens. The sailboat owner used to be able to repair most of the things on the vessel without assistance. Not any more. With computerization and miniaturization, many systems are too complicated for the average boat owner. With the installation of sealed units, repairs are often impossible and replacement is often necessary. This, of course, also means greater expense.

This is especially true with electrical and electronic systems. With almost every modern system on a boat there is some sort of electronic component. When you look at a vessel, do not get carried away with all the sophisticated systems she carries; instead, think of how you can repair these systems (or afford to have it done for you) when they break down.

ELECTRICAL

Some sailboats are very simple and only use a 12-volt direct current (12VDC) system for powering their navigation lights and radio or starting their engine. Others have complex circuitry with various charging systems, distribution panels and inverters. When looking at electrics, it doesn't matter how complicated, the primary check should be for **corrosion**. An insulated wire that looks good on the outside might have corrosion that infiltrated from the end terminals inside the protective cover.

Batteries

Any sailboat with an engine should have at least two separate batteries, one for starting (and backup) and one house battery for lights and accessories. Usually, with larger vessels, one sees separate battery banks, with the "house bank" being the largest (number of amp hours). Batteries can be different voltages, combined to make up the required 12VDC (most popular) or 24VDC.

In checking batteries, look for:

- Age and type (most common are lead acid wet and gel; marine starting or deep cycle). Check with the manufacturer for battery specifications—generally the wet batteries are more tolerant with charging and less expensive; the gel batteries are maintenance-free, need low-voltage charging and are more expensive. For all-around use, deep-cycle batteries are advised. The longevity can vary from 3 to 15 years, depending on type, number and thickness of plates.

- That it's secured in an acid-proof and leak-proof container.

- That it is placed in a well-ventilated area.

- If there is a main battery switch with sufficient capacity to handle a dead short of the electrical system.

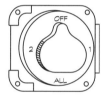 

Examples of main battery switches

Charging Systems

There are many excellent charging systems available for boats, and depending on the use, most sailboats carry at least two. Beware if the systems are other than "off the shelf" units. This does not mean there aren't good custom built charging systems out there. But if they are not protected properly, or correctly installed, one could run into a host of other problems such as additional corrosion and shortened battery life. Check the wiring diagrams or take them to someone who understands marine electrics.

- <u>Engine</u> - This is primarily a belt-driven alternator (can be more than one). It can vary in capacity from an average 30A to high output of 250A per hour. The latter will usually have a special 3 or

4 stage regulator and monitoring panel for the most rapid and efficient charging possible. The size of an alternator depends on the total charging need and battery capacity, i.e., number of amp hours used per day.

- Wind or water driven – This is a special alternator which will charge at low revolutions coupled to a propeller; it can charge up to 20A depending on speed. Normally, these systems are found in offshore cruising vessels.

- Solar panels – These are various sizes of thin panels using the reaction of sunlight on silicone or germanium crystals to produce an electric current. They are either self-regulating or, in the larger ones, have a separate voltage regulator. Each cell puts out about half a volt and they are connected in series to produce 14+ volts. Amperage is governed by size of the cells—the average is around 2.5 amps. The main advantage is long, almost maintenance-free life.

- Generator plant - This is normally 120VAC run by a small diesel or gasoline motor and coupled to a charger. They are found on larger vessels with many electrical accessories.

- Shore power charger – This automatically charges batteries when vessel is hooked up to 120VAC or 240VAC shore power.

When checking any of these systems, make sure they are built for a marine environment and located in protected areas. Again, look for **corrosion.**

Panels
Electrical panels can vary depending on the size and complexity of the system. When checking, important things to remember:

- There must be one main switch that isolates the power source completely.

- There should be enough separate circuits with switch breakers or fuses not to overload any one set of wires.

- Panels should be easily seen and accessible.

- It is preferable to have warning lights for critical circuits, i.e., bilge pumps and alarms.

- Have meters that indicate volts, amps, battery condition.

Electrical panel

Wiring

Marine standard wiring is double insulated (outer jacket with two insulated wires inside). Check and watch for:

- Wire size. Most normal circuits are #14 or #16. Battery wires and other high amperage circuits, i.e., electric anchor winch will have wires from #00 to #8.

- Wires. They must be stranded, not solid, to stand up better to vibration and movement; preferably marked for identification.

- Proper grounding of all circuits. (In many boats, you might find a copper ground bar to which everything is connected.)

- Wiring should be neat, secure and accessible—beware of loose ends, bare wires, jury rigs, and buried wiring.

- Connections should be soldered or connected with approved crimp-on fittings and well-insulated.

- Terminals or terminal boards should be protected with silicone spray or something similar.

Discussion

With electrical systems, you have to work backwards to see if the vessel you are looking at meets your requirements. Check to see how many items there are that use the boat's power supply. Calculate how many amp-hours (how many amps does each item draw, if it is marked in watts, divide it with the voltage of the power supply to arrive at the amperage, then multiply that by the average daily use in hours) are used on the vessel, daily or weekly. Then, look at the size of the batteries and if given a total amp-hour capacity, divide that in half to arrive at usable storage capacity. Sometimes, the stated capacity of the battery takes the 50% into account. With most batteries, the voltage drops below optimum after 50% has been consumed.

When you have the usable capacity and amp-hours required, you can find out how long you can "sail" the boat before starting the engine to charge the batteries. (This is unless you have some outside charging source like solar cells or wind generator.)

Check what the total charging capacity is on the vessel, taking into account the capability of the alternator(s) and regulator(s). For efficiency, it is advised to use the "smart" 3 or 4 stage regulators that monitor the batteries and provide the maximum charging rate. The older automotive types can take 2 or 3 times longer to charge the same size batteries. If you find that to keep your electrical appliances happy, you need to run the engine much longer than you want to, either look at alternate methods of charging, increase your charging capacity, or get rid of some of your appliances. Remember, that everything is a trade-off. If you increase the size of your alternator, you also increase the amount of horsepower necessary to drive it, taking it away from the power driving the propeller. If you have a small engine giving a shaft horse power output of 25, and the propeller size and pitch take up 20 of that for optimum performance, that leaves only 5 to run the alternator, water pump(s), and so forth. A large output alternator can easily use up to 5 horsepower under load.

With older vessels especially, owners add on appliances, wiring, and instruments over the years. Often, they are wired into the existing circuitry without paying attention to wire size, fuse capacity, etc. Sometimes wire runs are abandoned and new ones put in, leaving wires that go nowhere (sometimes still connected into the circuit), have loose ends, or are unidentified. This can be a nightmare for the new owner, and can lead to problems and even the loss of the boat in case of bilge pump failure, overheated wires causing a fire, and so forth. Often old circuits are hidden behind paneling which can make it worse. All wiring *has* to be accessible. When inspecting the electrical system be very conscientious and if not sure of a particular circuit or wire ask the owner, or trace it back to the beginning, even if it means removing panels or moldings. Pay particular attention to grounding circuits—they are often neglected as "not being important" but, in fact, the opposite is true.

PLUMBING

Similar to electric systems, plumbing can be simple (one or two manual freshwater pumps) or complicated (pressure hot and cold water, shower/tub, hot-water heating).

However, there are common elements in both:

- Water lines – They are usually plastic (reinforced or braided), polyurethane, or vinyl, rather than rigid copper or ABS. They need to withstand corrosion and vibration. All lines must be secured or protected; look for wear or chafe and proximity to sharp corners or objects.

- Clamps – They should be made of stainless steel (including pin) or another non-corrosive material. There should be high-impact, temperature-resistant plastic pressure fittings. Check for leaks. *All hoses to underwater through hull fittings must be double clamped.*

- Filters - All fresh and salt water pumps must have a filter on the suction side to prevent pump damage.

- <u>Gray water hoses</u> - Should be reinforced plastic (nylon, not steel, coil reinforcement). Bilge pumps should have fire resistant hoses, especially in the engine room.

- <u>Valves</u> - Through hull valves should have 90-degree shut-off, non-corrosive ball or cone type. Check for accessibility and ease of movement. If valves are bronze or grounded in a wooden or GRP vessel to prevent galvanic corrosion, **there must be lightning protection installed.**

- <u>Pumps</u> - Check for leaks both on the suction side (loss of prime) and the pressure side. If vessel has a pressure water system, check for secondary or manual backup system. The pressure side should have an accumulator tank to prevent surging and wear on the pump motor; check air bladder in tank.

- <u>Waste disposal</u> – This is increasingly becoming a requirement in protected waters. Check regulations in your area. Most types consist of a tank (built-in or portable bladder) made out of, or protected with, non-corrosive material. It usually has a pump and a Y-valve to select inboard or overboard disposal. Check for pump-out ability and for smell (usually indicates a leak or lack of maintenance). All hoses should be double clamped; it is preferable to have inspection plates on the tank for cleaning out.

Discussion

Plumbing systems are nearly as bad as electrical systems for having things added to them. Many older vessels have a myriad of pipes and hoses as the plumbing system was upgraded. Often during upgrades, the older plumbing was left in because it was impossible to remove. As long as it is clear which is in use and which abandoned, and the latter does not interfere with the new system or promote any boat deterioration (which can happen in wooden, steel or aluminum vessels), leaving it in is acceptable.

Through hull fittings under the waterline, shutoff valves, and their respective hoses are of primary importance since there is access to the water outside and failure of any could sink the boat. It has been mentioned that lightning protection is important for grounded fittings in wood and GRP boats. There have been instances where lightning has struck unprotected vessels with grounded fittings and blown the through hull fitting out of the hull, causing the vessel to sink. With ungrounded fittings, there would not be a readily accessible path for the lightning current to follow. Although, if any of the hoses have a steel coil reinforcement, there is a possibility the fitting is grounded, so using hose of this type with ungrounded fittings is not recommended.

By not grounding the through hulls, there is some danger of electrolysis attacking the fittings if the vessel is not adequately protected by sacrificial anodes (zincs). There have been instances where, in unsuitable shut-off valves, the zinc was "eaten away" out of the casting, leaving a friable substance that readily disintegrated when handled.

VENTILATION

The major cause for dry rot in a boat is lack of ventilation. This is especially true if the vessel is not moving, i.e., in a marina. Air must be able to enter and exit the vessel. The best method to check adequate ventilation is with your nose -- by smell.

Check:

• Port holes and/or hatches to make sure they open.

• For permanent vents (Dorade, mushroom, solar powered fans), There should be at least one per cabin;

• Openings or louvres in cupboard doors, lockers and other enclosed spaces;

• Engine-room ventilation. This is very important for efficient operation of engine and removal of fumes;

• That batteries are well ventilated to carry away explosive gasses.

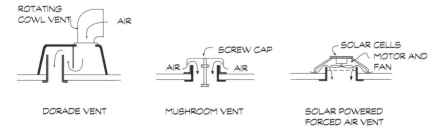

ROTATING COWL VENT   AIR

DORADE VENT

SCREW CAP
AIR   AIR
MUSHROOM VENT

SOLAR CELLS
MOTOR AND FAN
SOLAR POWERED FORCED AIR VENT

HEATING

Obviously heating depends on your home port or where you want to sail. In the higher latitudes where there is cold and humidity, the ability to heat is necessary. There are many different heaters available, and, to discuss them all in detail would require a separate book.

Some basic things of which to be aware and check:

- Is the vessel insulated and with what material (helps prevent condensation)? Some foam insulations are extremely flammable and can give off toxic fumes when ignited.

- Type of fuel and source. (Is it diesel, pressure kerosene, propane?)

- If the heater uses cabin air for combustion, what is the source of air? (Vented or exhausting heaters are better and safer than catalytic types.)

- With diesel or kerosene heaters, smell for leaks and check chimneys for soot build-up. (It could indicate inefficient operation, dirty burners, lack of air, or carburetor problems.)

- Propane heaters/furnaces must have gas sensors and other safety devices. Rigid lines must be well secured to prevent fatigue through vibration and flare fittings used at the connections.

- All heaters must have fireproof surrounds and deck head chimneys. (Check local fire regulations.)

Discussion

Ventilation and heating systems go hand in hand since, for the health of the boat, they both depend on having an adequate supply of moving air. There should not be any sealed areas leading to stagnant air, especially when the boat is not used during the winter. Still, humid air is a perfect environment for the proliferation of mildews, molds and rusts. Any indication of this probably means the existence of dry rot somewhere in the vessel.

TANKS

The main tanks found on a sailboat are fuel and water; others could include holding or waste tanks, hot water, hydraulic, propane, kerosene and separate day tanks for diesel heaters.

Engine fuel tanks can be made from stainless steel, black iron, GRP, high impact plastic. *Galvanized or non-ferrous tanks are not suitable since they may react to chemicals in the fuel.*

Check:

• Capacity and baffle plates for leaks, corrosion or deterioration.

• Fuel inlet and outlet (standpipe going down) and breather (vent). Vent should be on top of the tank—a drain plug on the bottom is allowed. If the outlet is on the bottom, there must be an easily accessible shut-off valve.

• Tank mounts. Are they adequate to take a potential knockdown or pitchpole?

• Fuel lines. Look for chafe or wear, flex lines must be flame-resistant.

• Paint. It is advisable that plastic and GRP tanks be painted with fire-resistant (intumescent) paint.

Water tanks

• Should be built from non-toxic material, i.e., stainless steel, GRP, ABS plastic, with baffle plates.

• Check capacity, leaks, breather.

• It is preferable to have inspection plates for cleaning.

• For offshore vessels, it is better to have several smaller tanks rather than one large tank in case of contamination.

• Some vessels may have a water maker. The usual type for small boats uses the osmosis principle, where water is forced with high pressure through a membrane, taking out the impurities. The manual versions only produce small amounts of water per hour (for survival). The motor-driven versions use a large amount of electrical power.

<u>Propane tanks</u> can be steel, stainless steel or aluminum.

- Tanks have date/number stamped. Check validity and when inspection is due.

- Especially in steel tanks, check bottom for corrosion.

- Look for valve leaks (by smell or use soapy water solution).

- Tanks must be in top-loading compartments with vent to outside on bottom.

Discussion

An important factor to remember when looking at a tank, is how difficult and expensive it would be to replace. In many vessels, tanks can be an integral part of the hull, i.e., part of the interior mold of the vessel, or they can be large and well built-in. In either case, to replace them would be almost impossible without a great deal of work. From this, one could surmise that the older the vessel the more suspect the tank, since it is probably the original one!! With steel tanks there will always be a certain amount of moisture present due to condensation, leading to corrosion inside. Flexible tanks, unless well protected, often suffer from chafe. GRP (fiberglass) tanks if not properly constructed, can crack or weep fuel through exposed fibers. Solid plastic ABS or high density polyethylene tanks are susceptible to ultra violet radiation causing them to become brittle, so they need to be protected from the sun. **Tanks have to be securely mounted; any vibration or movement could have disastrous results with broken lines or fittings. When looking at a tank, see if you can move it; if so, check for further damage.**

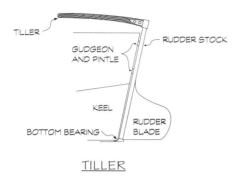

TILLER

For all steering systems, check bearings and stuffing box for rudder shaft (if any) for leaks and ease of movement. For transom-hung rudders, check the gudgeons and pintles for wear to ensure it is securely fastened.

Steering

The method of steering used in a sailboat is with a tiller or a wheel. Usually, a larger vessel uses the latter. The main reason for this is that a tiller is directly connected or fixed to the rudder shaft. Its length is related to the square footage of the rudder blade (resistance). A larger vessel with a large rudder would take a longer tiller to operate easily and, therefore, occupy more space in the cockpit area. Wheel steering uses some type of mechanical advantage with a quadrant or short tiller arm.

Wheel

■ **Cable** – It uses a roller chain, sprocket, sheaves and cable to move a quadrant attached to the rudder shaft.

• Check condition of chain and cable for wear, broken strands, or kinks.

• Look at the size and type of turnbuckles for take-up.

• Check end terminals for wear and corrosion.

• Inspect sheaves for lubrication and to ensure they're securely fastened.

• Check quadrant for wear, stress cracks, and alignment.

■ **Rack and pinion** – A wheel turns a pinion gear which, in turn, moves a toothed bar or rail connected to a tiller arm (can also be a worm gear with a push-pull rod).

- Check for wear on gear and teeth. (This causes a sloppy wheel.)
- Check the security of tiller arm, wear of pin and hole.

Hydraulic steering ram and tiller arm

■ **Hydraulic** – The wheel turns a manual pump which forces hydraulic oil to move a double-acting ram (piston in a hydraulic cylinder) connected to a tiller arm.

- Check air in system. (Turn the wheel hard over and feel for sponginess).
- Inspect for leaks. (pump seals, lines, connections, ram seals)
- Check size of lines. (Larger uses less friction.)
- Look at tiller arm for wear; inspect terminal pin and hole.

Tiller

- Check the condition of tiller for cracks, repairs, deterioration.
- Check ease of movement.
- Is there enough space in the cockpit?

<u>Autopilots (if applicable)</u>

Things to look for:

- Is it electric or wind operated? What is its age?

- What is the power draw?

- Check belts (if any) for wear or cracks and inspect electrical terminals for corrosion.

- In hydraulic systems, check location and condition of pump and motor (corrosion, leaks).

Discussion

There is no single, perfect, steering system for a boat, although a tiller for a smaller vessel probably comes close. The main advantages are its simplicity, ease of operation, inexpensive maintenance, and its nautical look! As soon as you get into wheel steering, it becomes complicated. The older method of using chain, cable and a quadrant, takes up quite a lot of space; the sheaves, cable, and gear head take continuous maintenance, and it can be noisy. Compared to a tiller, there are a lot of wear points, and often it is difficult to get at since the cable runs are usually placed in out-of-the-way locations.

The rack and pinion gear type takes up less space when a push/pull cable is used but, in larger vessels, this is not strong enough and a solid rod with universal connections and a tiller arm attached to the rudder shaft is used. This limits the placement of the steering system. However, it is a direct linkage with good rudder feel.

Hydraulic steering is probably the most popular among larger boats. The use of oil, pump and cylinder makes it a very powerful acting system, while the use of flexible lines makes it more versatile in locating the helm. The main objection that many sailors have is the lack of "feel" of the rudder. However, this is sometimes an advantage, since when leaving the wheel, it is automatically locked. All of these steering systems are able to support an autopilot.

Electronics

Although the meaning of the word refers to the "technology dealing with the behavior of electrons," in this guide it covers the wide field of radio, instrumentation, and aids to navigation. As with most items (other than some basic aids recommended to have on a boat, i.e., VHF radio, depth sounder), the remainder is personal preference, often dependent on how much you want to spend.

*Since **all** electronic devices use electric current, when doing your inspection, check for corrosion at any of the terminals, power, speaker, remote, antennas, etc. Most equipment faults can be traced to this area.*

Radio

VHF - Although two-way radios are not mandatory, it is advisable to have a VHF (very high frequency) radio for "line of sight" communication and local weather forecasts. In many countries, a *Restricted Radio Operator* certificate is required. It usually means taking a very short exam to check your understanding of operating the radio, especially in cases of emergency.

Things to look at:

- Check that the radio works, receiving and transmitting (Channel 16 is mandatory).

- Check that the radio is secured in a dry, protected location and is easily accessible.

- Examine the antenna type (3dB or 6dB) and location. (dB refers to the gain of the antenna. A 3dB sends out a broader pattern, so that when heeled over, part of the signal is still sent in a relatively horizontal direction and can be received. A 6dB antenna sends out a narrow pattern so that when heeled over a lot, most of the signal is sent up into the air or into the water. However, a 6dB signal will travel further than a 3dB signal if the antenna is upright.)

Additional radios you might find are:

- CB (citizens band);

- SSB (single-side band). This can be HF (high frequency) or VHF marine bands. The former may also have amateur radio bands (Ham). Other operator licenses may also be required;

- Radio telephones which use land-based or satellite-based communication, including weather fax, fax and email.

(Be sure to check what licenses, operation agreements/rentals are required.)

Instrumentation and aids to navigation

Depth sounder – This is also known as a "fish finder." Older models are usually a *flashing type* (a rapidly spinning wheel with a light). The *recording type* uses paper with a "graph" showing the bottom and because of its size, it is usually on larger vessels. All the newer sounders are *digital* or have a *scanning* capability showing underwater features on a screen, often in color. Some have *plotting* features as well.

GPS – The *Global Positioning System* determines longitude and latitude location using a satellite network. These can be self-contained handheld receivers or fixed with an external antenna. They also determine speed over the ground, return to man overboard, and other useful functions.

LORAN – This *LOng-range RAdio Navigation* gives your location using land-based transmitters; this is gradually being replaced with GPS and will be obsolete if and when governments turn off transmitters.

RADAR - *RAdio Direction And Range* detects objects by sending out radio waves which are reflected back. Over the last few years, RADAR units have become more affordable and compact in size. With an enclosed antenna (Radome), they are seen more often on smaller sailing vessels. Most popular units have a 16- or 24-mile range and only draw 2-4 amps of power. They all have an interface capability with an autopilot—LORAN or GPS.

<u>Chart Plotters</u> - They can take the place of paper navigational charts using *chart cartridges* electronically projected onto a screen. Zoom capability as well as waypoint storage and route projection are also included. Most units can interface with GPS and RADAR.

<u>Speed/Log</u> - This shows speed and total nautical miles travelled. It can be a digital or dial readout using a passive transducer or small paddlewheel projecting under hull in a transducer. The latter can foul with weed or the pin can wear out.

<u>Wind direction/Speed</u> - Most are similar to the speed/log unit having digital or dial readout and having some kind of sensor on the masthead.

<u>Electronic Compass</u> – This uses a fluxgate compass situated remote from the instrument in the center of the vessel and gives a digital readout of direction. This is often coupled with an autopilot and RADAR interface.

Discussion

The world of electronics -- radios, instrumentation, aids to navigation -- is expanding at an incredible rate. The choice of depth sounders, plotters, and location devices is almost limitless. Looking through any marine catalogue will often leave the new boat buyer somewhat bewildered. Probably, the main thing to remember is that all of these devices operate on electricity and therefore are vulnerable in a marine climate. Even the most waterproof, sealed unit will eventually be affected. Since many run off the main power supply of the vessel, they all add to the overall amp-hour usage, and when your battery dies, so do they. Certainly, have them on your vessel if your boat can support them. But, do not depend solely on these devices, they are aids—in other words, they are there to help you, not take your place. Make certain you know how to navigate without them or, at least be aware of the compass, the sextant (if offshore), the lead line and dead reckoning techniques.

Chapter 8
Looking at Critical Areas

If you like the looks of the boat, and perhaps glossed over the previous sections. . . **these are "must do's" —even if you have to get a friend to do it for you!**

- Look **under the sole** and **in lockers.** These will often indicate if there are any problems with construction or maintenance (again "out-of-sight, out-of-mind"). Check for any strong smells, dampness or soft spots that could indicate dry rot or leaks. Feel the hull where the bulkhead is attached for any sharp fibers or loose glass (in GRP boats), any illogical spaces or cracks (in wooden boats), and uneven or no welds or lumps (in metal boats), cracks, voids, or bare metal (in ferro-cement boats). These usually indicate sloppy workmanship and, therefore, be extra wary in further examination of the vessel.

- Check the **hull/deck joint.** If it is hidden in the living areas, look in the lazarrette or anchor chain locker. Is it a mechanical (bolted and/or screwed) joint or glassed/welded together? In some cases, one might find both. Is there any indication of leaks (i.e., discoloration) or movement?

- Carefully check the **rudder** and **rudder stock.** Are the bearings tight, any straps secure, rudder blade well-fastened to the rudder shaft? Is the shaft of sufficient diameter? Does it *look* strong? Is the tiller, tiller arm or quadrant secure on the shaft? *(They must be keyed and clamped.)*

- If the vessel has a **bolted-on keel**, check the condition of the bolts. If any feel loose or show *any sign* of corrosion, have one removed for further inspection. Do not take chances, keels have been known to drop off! When the boat is out of the water, you can check the keel (or ballast) joint. If there is a small "crack," don't be alarmed, there is often some movement caused by expansion and contraction. A large one may indicate a loose keel or rot (in a wooden boat).

- Faulty **through hull fittings** or **valves** can sink a boat. Try to find one that has as few underwater fittings as possible. Check that they meet marine standards, are well caulked and fastened (or welded). Valves *must* move freely. If there is any doubt, while out of the water, remove the retaining nut and take out the insides to check for pitting or other corrosion.

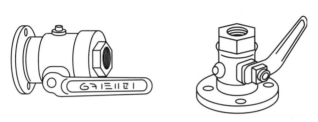

Some typical marine valves

- Check the **ground circuits**. Often people will check positive terminals and ignore ground terminals. *Remember, that some of the most serious corrosion damage in a boat is caused by stray currents.* They can use moist wood, bilge water, or metal as a pathway to the nearest ground, teaming up with the low voltage of electrolysis to do serious damage.

- At the same time as checking ground circuits, check the **zincs.** These are the sacrificial anodes which slowly disintegrate by the low voltage created by having dissimilar metals in seawater. *If there are no zincs, immersed fittings will start to disintegrate beginning with the least noble on the galvanic scale.*

- Look at **protection circuits and alarms**. This depends on the vessel and what fuel is used aboard (engine, cooking, heating).

   - If propane is used, you must have sensors located low in the boat (bilges, sole) coupled to an audible alarm and automatic shut-off valve on the propane tanks.

   - If gasoline is used for the engine, you must have a blower (turned on several minutes before starting the engine) and a fume detector in the engine room coupled to an audible alarm.

- It is a good idea to have a high-water sensor and alarm in the bilge. Or, at least, have some indicator that shows when the bilge pump is operating.

- Although not necessary, it may save you a lot of expense if there are engine alarms in the vessel, i.e., high engine temperature, low oil pressure.

- Installation of smoke alarms and heat sensors in the cooking area, accommodation areas and engine room are also a good idea, although not required unless you are a charter vessel or carrying paying passengers.

• **Bilge pumps** can save your boat. There should be at least one automatic 12VDC pump in the bilge. *This should be of sufficient size to pump incoming water from a broken through hull fitting or hose, until the hole can be blocked or clamped off.* In addition to an electric pump(s), there must be a manual one as well. Other pumps you may run into are engine or hydraulic driven, usually through a magnetic or manual clutch. These are generally of high-volume and found on larger vessels. Some boats have portable, high-volume, electric bilge pumps, either DC or AC, which come complete with discharge hose and extension cord. When looking at bilge pumps, *make certain they and any other automatic switches work.* (Check to see the water coming out of the end!)

A variety of float switches, electric and manual bilge pumps

- **Safety gear and extinguishers** - In most countries, the requirements for safety equipment are stated in the <u>Coast Guard Safety Regulations</u>. Check what is required before you look at the vessel. Depending on the size and use of the boat, this would include items such as:

  - Number and type of portable fire extinguishers. *Make sure they are securely mounted and have inspection tags with the expiration date.*

  - Fixed extinguishing systems. *These are generally found in larger vessels, especially in the engine compartment; again, check if inspected and meet the requirements.*

  - Flares. *Check type, number and expiration date.*

  - Horn or other sound device.

  - Life rings and heaving line.

  - Personal flotation devices -- *life jackets, or similar.*

  - Navigation lights. *Check that they work and have the proper size bulb.*

  - Bilge pumps.

  - Radar reflector. *These are especially necessary for non-metallic vessels.*

  - Emergency communications -- *radios, EPIRB or other automatic emergency transmitters*

  - First-aid kit.

  - Anchor and rode.

  - Dinghy or tender. *It can be hard (fiberglass, wood) or an inflatable.*

  - Life-raft. *This is primarily for either passenger vessels or those going offshore. Check that it is of sufficient size for the crew and has been inspected and checked within the expiration date.*

- The word **haul-out** has been used a number of times throughout this guide. It means checking the vessel out of the water. After viewing the boat inside and out, while afloat, arrangements should be made with the owner(s) to haul out the vessel. The responsibility of taking her out is that of the owner(s) or broker. Usually, the interested buyer pays the cost which is taken off the purchase price if a deal is made.

Haul-out on a travel lift

Discussion

This section has nothing to do with the special things or comforts that make each boat unique. It is only concerned with the structural integrity and the safety of the vessel. These are items that have to be looked at, and could make the difference whether further examination of the boat is warranted. In some sense this could be the first section of this guide, except it demands some basic knowledge of sailboat construction which is contained in the earlier chapters.

If the vessel you are looking at does not satisfactorily meet the conditions mentioned above, it does not mean automatic rejection, unless the structure has deteriorated beyond repair. It does mean that unless these items are replaced, corrected, repaired, or installed, the vessel does not conform to basic safety requirements and you could encounter serious problems in the future.

It is important to remember that the installation of protection circuits, alarms, and safety gear does not preclude using common sense. A regular operational check and maintenance program is absolutely necessary. Know how to use the fire extinguishers, flares, radios, and so forth. Have the alarms, if electrical, be independent of the boat's power supply.

Chapter 9
The Test Sail

At this point, you have examined the boat thoroughly inside and out, above and below, and you are ready to sign on the dotted line. However, you don't know yet, beautiful that she is, whether this boat will meet your expectations moving through the water. *This is the final test.* You need to make the arrangements to take her for a sail. Remember not to pick the sunniest, windless day to try the boat out— every boat is great in the sun on glass-smooth water! Do not pick a day with 35 knots of wind on the nose and four-foot waves either, unless you are young or a masochist. When you leave the dock or buoy, you will more than likely be under power. If leaving a crowded marina, it is a perfect opportunity to see how the vessel responds when avoiding other boats.

As you head out into the bay you can check the engine and look for:

- How noisy is the boat?

- Are there any strange vibrations or thumping noises at a certain RPM (which may indicate a worn cutless bearing, unbalanced propeller, or bent shaft)?

- Is there an excessive exhaust smell?

- What is the color of the exhaust. (Black can indicate too much fuel, which could mean fuel pump or injector problems in diesels. Blue exhaust is usually burning oil, which might mean a problem with rings, valves or pistons.)

- How comfortable is the boat under power? What are the conditions inside?

- Check the engine gauges for oil pressure, water temperature and alternator charging rate?

- Check how the navigation instruments work -- speed log, wind speed, radar, auto pilot, etc. Is there any electrical interference when the engine is running?

Try the vessel at different engine speeds (RPM), and notice the difference in any of the above checks.

By now, the owner is probably getting the sail covers off, winch handles out and running rigging ready. You should:

- Check on how it is done (you might even want to help). Are there any difficulties, any machinery or hatches in the way?

The boat turns into the wind, the engine slows down and the main sail is raised. As the vessel turns across the wind and the foresail(s) goes up, *the boat is starting to sail!*

Downwind sailing

Off goes the engine, and you realize how grand the silence is, as she slips along at a slight heel and easy motion . . . a sailboat!

From this moment, as you place your hands on the wheel or tiller, the boat is yours—the rest is only a formality.

However, before sailing off into the sunset:

- Try the boat at different points of sail.
- See how she responds to steering. Does she hold course easily or wander off?
- When coming about, is it smooth or does she end up in irons?
- How does she behave when the wind changes or under different wave conditions?
- Try the autopilot, especially if it works on wind direction.

Make a day of it. Don't decide until you have brought her back and docked. Take another look, and if you feel that you want to go out again, do so!

Chapter 10
Looking at the Price

After the euphoria wears off of finding the boat you want, it can be a letdown to discuss the actual purchase of the vessel. It is very seldom that the asking price of the seller coincides with what the buyer is willing to pay. There are a number of factors that need to be looked at, the first one being the legal status of the vessel.

Registration vs. licensing

This was briefly mentioned under Chapter 2, Looking at the Boat, but warrants further discussion. Probably the most important thing to remember is that *licensing does not necessarily imply ownership or title*. It only means that the vessel has a number and is registered with a municipal, provincial or state-run department.
The license usually:
- expires annually or every couple of years and therefore is not a permanent identification of the vessel;
- is generally inexpensive but can vary greatly depending on where acquired;
- does not require an inspection or viewing of the vessel;
- can be applied for by anyone, not necessarily the owner;
- is generally regarded as a type of tax.

Registering a vessel is a more complicated and expensive procedure in most instances. It usually implies the involvement of a national or federal department. Under international law, a vessel on the high seas is required to have a nationality, so for boats going offshore, registration is normally required. Registration documents the vessel; there is a procedure of name application and approval, measuring the vessel for gross and registered tonnage, and permanently marking the boat for identification purposes.
The advantages of registration are:
- Establishment of ownership, often as the number of shares in the vessel (in most countries only citizens can apply for boat registration);
- It gives "good title" to the vessel that cannot be overturned by

the holder of former interest (unless that interest was noted at time of purchase);

- It gives the vessel national protection on the high seas or in foreign ports;
- It is much easier to acquire a mortgage for the vessel, (mortgages and encumbrances are listed on the registration);
- It often adds value to the vessel since the buyer is assured of "good title";
- It is a once-only procedure, although there are additional forms (and costs) for registration of transfers, changing the name of the vessel, boat survey and so on. Registration can also take a fair length of time, depending on backlog.

There are exceptions, for example, registering the vessel at "a port of convenience," usually done for tax purposes. In countries like Belize, Antigua, and Panama to name a few, there are no application restrictions and registration can often be done by fax the same day.

Boat Broker vs. Private Seller

Like real estate, in most cases people who sell their boat use the services of a broker. This is usually because of their time limitations to show the vessel to prospective buyers. Often the seller can leave the boat with the broker at his docks, making it more available. This is sometimes cheaper because the seller does not have to pay moorage costs. Of course, again like selling real estate, the broker gets a percentage of the selling price.

Other possible advantages of using a broker:

- He looks after the vessel and presents her to the buyer in best light possible.
- He does minor or obvious repairs before selling.
- Although not having as intimate a knowledge of the boat as the owner, the broker can sometimes be more objective in presenting the vessel.
- Like a realtor, he assists in the arrangement of financing and the necessary paperwork, and can check ownership, encumbrances, liens, etc.

However, just because there is a broker, do not assume there is clear title! Check the paperwork; if you don't understand, ask.

71

If you deal with the owner directly, you will probably learn more about the vessel. This is especially true if the boat is "home built." Often the owner could be the builder giving you a wealth of knowledge about the construction and subsequent history of the vessel.

Other advantages of buying from the owner could be:

- It is usually easier "to make a deal" depending on how anxious he or she is to sell. If they wait, they will still have to pay moorage and keep up the maintenance of the vessel.
- Sometimes, if the owner feels the boat is going to a good home, the price could be reduced. Remember that an owner has an emotional investment as well as a monetary value in the vessel; this can work for, as well as against, the buyer.

Price? What price?

When you consider the price of a boat, four separate values come into play. It is important to understand the significance of all four.

Seller's or asking price

This is often a somewhat biased and inflated value based on the initial cost of buying, or constructing the boat, plus the cost of adding equipment or upgrading the vessel over the years. Multiply that by the emotional attachment and all the "good times" onboard and you have what the owner thinks the boat is worth.

Market price

This would be the average price of similar type vessels for sale at any one time. It can fluctuate quite a lot depending on how many boats are on the market, the demand, economic climate and even the time of year. Usually post-sailing season is a better time to buy than pre-season.

Replacement price

How expensive is it to replace the vessel, to either buy or build another just like it? This is usually the highest value, especially dealing with custom-built boats, since it relates to labor and material costs. A boat built 10 years ago costs a lot less than one built now.

Buyer's price/Offer

This is what you are prepared to pay for the vessel. After examining the vessel and going over the checklist, be prepared to discuss any faults or inadequacies with the owner or broker. Calculate the cost to repair/replace these inadequacies and deduct that off the market price to arrive at your offer. If it is a fair one, it will usually be accepted, otherwise you will have to do some more negotiating—or look for another boat.

Financing

After agreeing on a price, and you haven't got the cash, how will you pay for it?

Trades

Some boat sellers will trade their vessel for a house or property of equal value. This can be very beneficial for both parties by saving a considerable amount of money on sales tax. Of course this would not work too well if a broker was involved, unless both parties agreed to pay him a commission.

Sometimes a seller will take a trade as down payment, perhaps a smaller boat or vehicle. Items such as pianos, stocks & bonds, labor or professional services have also been used to reduce the full price. If you are so inclined and have something to trade, discuss it.

Owner financing

Some boat sellers will carry the financing wholly or in part. The former is quite rare, since often the boat has been put up for sale to acquire the money, either to buy a larger vessel, or put it towards something else completely different. Partial financing is much more frequent. Ask.

Other financing

If financing is necessary, the buyer usually goes to a bank or other financial institution. It is sad to say that on the whole, financing a boat is still regarded as more of a risk than financing a car or a house. A number of reasons have been put forward, the extreme one being that when one purchases a boat, there is the possibility of that person sailing off into the sunset. The more acceptable one is that all the additional costs one can accumulate such as moorage, maintenance, insurance, fuel, etc. can add substantially to a monthly payment. Boat mortgages still fall under the heading of "chattel mortgages" and therefore a buyer cannot take advantage of the usually lower rates available when buying a house. With most financial institutions a 10% down payment is necessary before one will qualify for financing.

Rates and amortization can vary depending on:

* Where you go;
* How much they want your business;
* Amount of mortgage;
* Past credit experience;
* How much other business you do at that branch.

Discussion

It is definitely worth shopping around for a lending institution before you even start to look for a boat. Some banks or credit unions are set up to do boat financing (usually because there are a number of sailors on the staff) and can do most of the legal work on the premises saving the buyer the extra costs. Most financial institutions give preference to registered vessels. All title and encumbrance information is readily available without doing lien and ownership searches. A recent survey of the vessel by a qualified, acceptable marine surveyor (make sure of the latter) is almost always a requirement.

Much has been said about marine surveyors in other publications. If you are financing or insuring the vessel you won't have much choice; you will have to have the vessel surveyed sooner or later. Choosing one can be difficult since on the whole it is an unregulated body. There are associations that "self-regulate" but belonging to one doesn't necessarily ensure you are getting a good surveyor, just as not belonging to an association doesn't necessarily make one a poor surveyor. Go by past experience and question the surveyor about his credentials. The best surveyor has a wide range of experience in not only designing boats, but also in building them and operating them in various conditions.

Conclusions

This guide is exactly that: an aid to help you make a decision about buying a used sailboat. This is a very personal experience for most people. Although you still might want to use the services of a marine surveyor (or might have to if you are financing the vessel) check the surveyor's certification or registration, and ask for references. Lastly, don't underestimate what *you* feel—your gut reaction—about the boat. If you have followed this guide and used the checklist, trust your intuition and the answer of whether or not to buy that particular boat will be there. The first boat, or even the 20th boat, you look at may not be yours, but somewhere she is waiting—you can be sure of that!

Glossary

anodized - metal, especially aluminum, is covered with a protective oxide layer by electrolysis

antiskid - pattern or granular material on decks to prevent slipping or skidding

armature - metal framework

baffle plates - plates inside tanks used to restrain motion of a liquid

bilge - lowest part inside a hull

bitter end - the inboard end of an anchor line

blocks - a metal, wood or plastic case in which one or more sheaves are fitted, used to increase mechanical advantage of ropes or change direction

bosun's chair - (boatswain's chair) a short board secured in a bridle used to lift a person up the mast

catalytic - a heater that has no exhaust or air intake, but uses a device that changes harmful gasses to less harmful ones

chine - joint between the side and bottom of a boat

crazing - fine surface cracks

cutless bearing - type of bearing on the outside end of a propeller shaft tube

delamination - separation of layers

displacement - amount of water displaced by a floating object (boat)

Dorade vents - type of adjustable deck vent that allows air in but keeps water out

electrolysis - the decomposition of a substance by application of an electric current—in marine applications, this current is initiated by dissimilar metals immersed in seawater

fairing - process of streamlining or smoothing the exterior of a boat

fluxgate compass - an electronic compass which measures the relative strength of magnetic fields passing through two wire coils and through this process deduces the earth's magnetic field

frames - "ribs" of a boat running from keel to deck forming the skeleton or shape and reinforcement of the hull

freewheel - propeller and shaft allowed to turn freely, caused by movement through water

furling - rolling up (or reducing) a sail

galley - kitchen on a boat

galvanic corrosion -corrosion caused by electrolysis

gimbals - suspension system used to keep equipment level; i.e., lamps, compasses, cooking stoves

gudgeon and pintle - pintle is the vertical pin attached to the leading edge of a rudder and fits into an eye bolted on the transom or sternpost; holds rudder in place

halyard - lines or wires used to haul up or lower sails or yards

head - ship's toilet

heat exchanger - type of "radiator" where heat or cold from one fluid is transferred or exchanged to another

holding tank - waste tank

interface - interaction between two or more systems

in irons - vessel allowed to come up into the wind and lose way through the water so that she will not turn on either tack

keyed - a piece of metal, usually rectangular bar shape, inserted in a keyway between two other pieces of metal, thus securing them

knockdown – the vessel is "knocked" over sideways by wind or a large wave, sometimes with the mast touching the water, or even further

lazarrette - compartment set aside for storage, usually located in the aft end of a vessel

log book - a book in which the boat's records are kept

lug sail - a four-sided sail set on a yard; similar to a gaffsail

mast boot - a waterproof cover where a keel-stepped mast goes through a deck

monocoque - structure where the frame is integral with the body

mortar - mixture of lime, cement, sand and water

mushroom vent - overhead, round air vent, with an opening screw top

osmosis - passage of a liquid through a semi-permeable partition, cover or membrane

oxidation - process of oxygen combining with another material producing an oxide; i.e., rust

pinion gear - a small gear that engages a bigger one, often at right angles

pitchpole – the vessel is turned over end-for-end, usually by a large wave or wind which buries the bow in the water and the momentum carries the boat over

quadrant - a quarter of a circle's circumference casting secured to the rudder post

raw water - seawater, or water not contained in the vessel's water tanks

reef points - short lengths of rope used to tie down a reef when shortening sail

rigging - all ropes, wires and chains used on a boat

rode - rope

roller furling - apparatus to roll up or furl a sail from a remote location

rope clutch - a device for holding or releasing a rope

rudder stock - upright member connecting the rudder blade to the steering mechanism

running rigging - all rigging used in the raising or lowering of sails and yards

sheave - a grooved wheel

sheets - rope attached to the clew (lower point) of a sail for securing or controlling it

shrouds - set of ropes or cables forming part of the standing rigging giving lateral support to the mast

sole - deck (floor) of the cabin

spinnaker pole - pole for pushing out the tack of a spinnaker sail

standing rigging - all rigging used to support masts, yards and bowsprit

stays - set of ropes or cables forming part of the standing rigging giving fore and aft support to the mast

stringer - longitudinal structural member (in a hull)

swaged - fastening of one metal part to another very high pressure i.e. turnbuckle to a wire shroud

tang - projection (on the mast) to which the shrouds or stays are attached

thrust bearing - a bearing secured to the hull which would take the fore and aft load or thrust of a propeller shaft

transom - aft end of a vessel

waypoint - a stopping place or co-ordinates for each stage of an ocean journey

yard - a wood or metal spar which supports a sail

Y valve - a two-way diverter valve

zincs - sacrificial anodes to prevent galvanic corrosion of immersed fittings

About the Author

Karel Doruyter is a registered marine surveyor and has been a sailboat enthusiast for more than 30 years. During his lifetime he has designed, constructed and maintained boats for himself as well as others. He has sailed his own boats in the coastal waters of Western Canada, the United States, and Australia as well as offshore. At present he lives in British Columbia and sails a cruising catamaran he designed and built.

For more information

For those who wish to do more in-depth reading about sailing, the following excellent nautical references are recommended: Chapman Piloting by Elbert S. Maloney; Royce's Sailing Illustrated; The Proper Yacht by Arthur Beiser; The Sailing Handbook by John Davies; Cruising Under Sail by Eric G. Hiscock; An Introduction to Sailing by Peter Blake and David Pardon; Handbook of Offshore Cruising by Jim Howard; Sails: The Way They Work by Derek Harvey; Multihulls Offshore by Rob James, and Multihull Voyaging by Thomas Firth Jones.

Buyer's Checklist

(Photocopy and use while viewing a boat.)

Size of vessel:

length _____

beam _____

draught _____

tonnage _____

Material: _____

_____

_____

_____

Distinguishing characteristics:

_____

_____

_____

_____

Sail rig, number of sails,

self-furling: _____

_____

_____

_____

Asking price: _____

Visual condition: _____

_____

_____

History of vessel, age, where built, etc.:

_____

_____

_____

_____

_____

_____

_____

_____

_____

_____

_____

_____

_____

_____

_____

_____

_____

Condition of hull, any deterioration or repairs:

Cracks: _____

Blisters: _____

Paint or gelcoat: _____

Corrosion: _____

Insulated:

Condition of deck, any deterioration or repairs:

Adequate layout:

Deck equipment:

_____

_____

_____

Number and condition of hatches:

Material and condition of mast(s) and boom(s):

_____

_____

_____

Material and condition of standing rigging:

_____

_____

_____

Material and condition of running rigging:

_____

_____

_____

Anchor winch:

Anchors:

Chain-locker condition: _____

Suitable interior layout: _____

_____

_____

Galley equipment:

_____

_____

_____

Condition of head:

_____

Type of toilet:

_____

Holding tank:

_____

_____

Number of cabins (berths):

Location and condition of engine compartment:

Type and model of engine:

_____

_____

No. of hours: _____

Condition and last servicing:

_____

_____

No. and type of filters:

_____

_____

Type of cooling:

Appearance when running:

_____

_____

Exhaust:

Noise:
Gauges:_____

Size and condition of prop. shaft:

_____

_____

Condition of stuffing box (leaks):

Size and condition of propeller:

_____

_____

Appearance of electrical system (type, wiring):

_____

_____

_____

Type, number and age of batteries:

_____

_____

_____

_____

_____

_____

_____

_____

Ventilated: _____

Container: _____

Charging system: _____

_____

_____

_____

_____

Electrical panels, breakers, fuses: _____

_____

_____

Location:

_____

_____

Condition of plumbing system: _____

_____

_____

Condition of hose clamps:

Filters:

Valves (type, condition):

Adequate ventilation:

Type: _____

_____

Heating (type and condition): _____

_____

_____

_____

Adequate exhaust and air availability: _____

_____

Number, type and material of tanks: _____

_____

_____

_____

_____

Location: _____

_____

Vented: _____

Type and condition of steering equipment:

_____

_____

_____

_____

Autopilot: _____

Number and type of radios:

Condition (working):

_____

_____

Other electronic equipment and condition:

Depth sounder:

LORAN:

GPS:

RADAR:

Plotters:

_____

Speed/Log:

_____

Wind direction/speed:

_____

Electronic compass:

Other:

Any unexplainable features:

_____

_____

_____

_____

_____

Condition of rudder and stock:

_____

_____

Condition of keel (bolts):

_____

_____

_____

Through hull valves open and close freely: _____

_____

Adequate ground circuits:

Type and condition of alarms:

_____

_____

_____

Capacity and condition of bilge pumps:

_____

_____

_____

_____

Automatic/manual:

_____

_____

_____

_____

_____

Fire extinguishers (type):

Location:

Last inspected:

Flares (number, type):

_____

Expiration date:

Sound device:

Life rings/heaving line:

PFD: Radar reflector: _____

EPIRB:

First aid kit:

Dinghy or tender:

Life raft:

Other:

_____

_____

_____

Hauled out:

Anti-fouling: _____

_____

Performance under power:

_____

_____

_____

_____

_____

Performance under sail: _____

_____

_____

_____

General remarks:

_____

_____

_____

_____

_____

_____

_____

_____

_____

_____

_____

_____

Enjoy these other adventure books from FineEdge.com

The Arctic to Antarctica
Cigra Circumnavigates the World
Mladen Sutej
The dramatic account of the first circumnavigation of the North and South American continents.

Cape Horn
One Man's Dream,
One Woman's Nightmare
Réanne Hemingway-Douglass
"This is the sea story to read if you read only one." —McGraw Hill, International Marine Catalog

Trekka Round the World
John Guzzwell
"John Guzzwell is an inspiration to all blue-water sailors."—*Wooden Boat*
"A classic of small boat voyaging."
—*Pacific Yachting*

Final Voyage of the Princess Sophia
Did they all have to die?
Betty O'Keefe and
Ian Macdonald
This story explores the heroic efforts of those who answered the SOS, at first to save and later to recover the bodies of those lost at sea.

For our full catalog check our website: www.FineEdge.com

Destination Cortez Island
A sailor's life along the BC Coast
June Cameron
A nostalgic memoir of the lives and times of coastal pioneers—the people and their boats, that were essential in the days when the ocean was the only highway.

Arctic Odyssey
Len Sherman
The account of *Dove III*'s epic voyage through the Northwest Passage—one of the first west-to-east single-year passages on record.

GPS Instant Navigation
A Practical Guide from Basics to Advanced Techniques
Kevin Monahan and Don Douglass
"Helps get more from your navigation."—*Pacific Yachting*
"I strongly recommend this book."—John Neal, Bluewater sailor, *Mahina Tiare*

Proven Cruising Routes for the Inside Passage to Alaska
Don Douglass and Kevin Monahan
All the waypoints for the major routes from Seattle to Ketchikan.

Exploring the San Juan and Gulf Islands

Cruising Paradise of the Pacific Northwest

Don Douglass and Réanne Hemingway-Douglass

Contributors: Anne Vipond, Peter Fromm, &Warren Miller

"Another masterpiece in the exploring series . . . "

Exploring the South Coast of British Columbia

Second Edition

Gulf Islands and Desolation Sound to Port Hardy and Blunden Harbour

Don Douglass and Réanne Hemingway-Douglass

"Clearly the most thorough, best produced and most useful [of the guides] available . . . particularly well thought out and painstakingly researched."
—NW Yachting

Exploring the North Coast of British Columbia

Blunden Harbour to Dixon Entrance, including the Queen Charlotte Islands

Don Douglass and Réanne Hemingway-Douglass

Describes previously uncharted Spiller Channel and Griffin Passage, the stunning scenery of Nakwakto Rapids and Seymour Inlet, Fish Egg Inlet, Queens Sound, and Hakai Recreation Area.

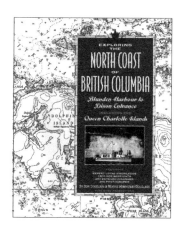

For our full catalog check our website: www.FineEdge.com

Exploring Southeast Alaska
Dixon Entrance to Skagway
Don Douglass and
Réanne Hemingway-Douglass
Over 1500 anchor sites in Alaska's
breathtaking southeastern archipelago;
for pleasurable cruising to thousands of
islands and islets, deeply-cut fjords,
tidewater glaciers and icebergs.

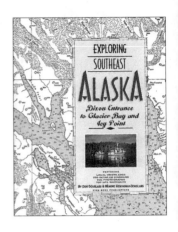

Exploring Vancouver
Island's West Coast
Second Edition
Don Douglass and
Réanne Hemingway-Douglass
With five great sounds, sixteen major
inlets, and an abundance of spectacular
wildlife, the largest island on the west
coast of North America is a cruising
paradise.

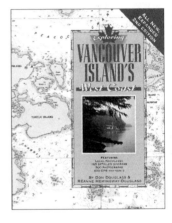

Exploring the
Marquesas Islands
Joe Russell
"A must reference for those wanting to
thoroughly enjoy their first landfall on the
famous Coconut Milk Run."—Earl Hinz,
author, *Landfalls of Paradise—Cruising
Guide to the Pacific Islands*

FineEdge.com
Phone 360-299-8500 • email: mail@FineEdge.com
For our full catalog check our website: www.FineEdge.com